HOW TO TALK FOOTBALL

by Arthur Pincus
illustrated by Taylor Jones

Dembner Books • New York

Dembner Books
Published by Red Dembner Enterprises Corp., 1841 Broadway, New York, N.Y. 10023
Distributed by W. W. Norton & Company, Inc., 500 Fifth Avenue, New York, N. Y. 10110

Copyright © 1984 by Arthur Pincus and Taylor Jones All rights reserved. No part of this book may be reproduced in any form without permission in writing from the publisher, except by a reviewer who wishes to quote brief passages in connection with a review written for inclusion in a magazine, newspaper, or broadcast.

Printed in the United States of America.

Library of Congress Cataloging in Publication Data

Pincus, Arthur.
    How to talk football.

    1. Football—United States—Terminology.   2. Football players—United States—Language (new words, slang, etc.)
3. English language—Terms and phrases.   4. English language—Jargon.   I. Title.
GV959.P585   1984   796.332′0973   84-11337
ISBN 0-934878-41-2 (pbk.)

CONTENTS

Introduction	5
Lexicon: From Alley Oop to Zone	13
Nicknames	83

Profiles: Twelve Men Who Have Enriched The Game of Football

WALTER CAMP	91
KNUTE ROCKNE	95
GEORGE HALAS	99
RED GRANGE	103
VINCE LOMBARDI	107
JIM BROWN	111
TOM LANDRY	115
JOE NAMATH	119
JOHN RIGGINS	123
LAWRENCE TAYLOR	127
JOHN MADDEN	131
LESTER HAYES	135

Index	139

For Ellen,
who talks about
other things.

INTRODUCTION

It was a Sunday afternoon in late January. Do you know where 100 million Americans were? Well, if it was Sunday, January 22, 1984 100 million or more of them were in front of television sets watching the Los Angeles Raiders defeat the Washington Redskins in Super Bowl XVIII. They were listening to Pat Summerall and John Madden describe the action on the field at Tampa Stadium and they were all part of the American ritual known as professional football.

Football is a Sunday event all over the United States. Wake up. Have breakfast. Read the Sunday newspaper. Then settle down in front of a television set to watch the day's pro football games (with perhaps a friendly wager to add to your rooting interest).

For Super Bowl Sunday, the interest is focused on one place and one game. But throughout the late summer, fall, and early winter the words and actions of the game of football are cast all over America. From the father tossing a football to his son; to sandlot games on rocky fields; to high school games that involve entire towns; to college games played in huge campus stadiums; to the highly technical, highly crafted big-paying pro game. For three-and-a-half months a year football is America.

When a group of student protestors against the Vietnam War congregated in front of the White House during the Richard Nixon administration, the President came out to talk with some of them. He talked not politics, but football. When Marcus Allen of the Los Angeles Raiders dazzled the Washington Redskins and all those viewers with his running in Super Bowl XVIII, President Reagan was on the telephone to the winners' locker room as soon as the Raiders arrived.

"That was a wonderful win," Mr. Reagan said to Coach Tom Flores. "But you've given me some problems. I've already gotten a call from Moscow. They think Marcus Allen is a new secret weapon. They insist we dismantle it. They've given me an idea about that team of yours. If you would turn them over to us, we'd put them in silos and we wouldn't have to build the MX missile."

Marcus Allen and the rest of the Raiders are not going to find themselves ensconced in any missile silos in Utah. But America is sure to keep hearing its political leaders talking football. Why not? It's fun.

Where and when did football begin finding its place in American culture? Dating back to the 1600s there are traces of games that involved kicking a ball. But the wellspring of football would have to be a game played between teams from Princeton and Rutgers Universities at Rutgers in New Brunswick, New Jersey. The date was November 6, 1869, and few of those 100 million who watched Super Bowl XVIII would recognize or name the game played that day as football. But the game at Rutgers was the forerunner of Super Bowl XVIII as surely as the game played with peach baskets in a Springfield, Massachusetts gymnasium in 1891 was the forerunner of this year's NBA final.

The game played at Rutgers was something that wasn't quite football or soccer as we now know them. But the two schools were able to agree on a set of rules that enabled the intercollegiate competition. Rutgers won the first game, six goals to four. The following week the teams met again, this time at Princeton. As the home team Princeton was able to make a rules change that helped it win by eight goals to none. Rutgers did not win another game against Princeton until 1938.

There were three games in 1870, when Columbia University entered the fray. But there was a problem. The game was too rough and the colleges refused to allow their students to play football at all in 1871. In 1872 the fourth university to take up the game joined in as some rules changes made football a little safer. The university was Yale and the brains and brawn that Yale brought to the sport ensured that football would be played forever.

On Yale's fifth varsity team was a scrawny freshman named Walter Camp. It was Camp who took football out of the realm of a chaotic pushing and shoving match and changed it into a game of speed, strength, and strategy. He invented the down; he devised the scrimmage, which gave teams ball possession; and he designed the field. Those are just the most noted contributions of his 50-year career. Through the years football always turned towards Yale and Camp for inspiration and innovation.

When Knute Rockne was asked where he got the shift his Notre Dame teams used so effectively, he responded, "Where everything else in football came from. Yale."

When a coach named Harry Mehre was at Georgia in the 1930s he said, "I'd rather beat any team in the country than Yale. For to me and most of us, Yale means American football."

And Fielding (Hurry Up) Yost, whose Michigan team played in the first Rose Bowl, said, "Walter Camp and Yale mean football. Yale was the first to have the true feel of the game—a game which means spirit, body contact, and team play, all the finest elements of competition. Many others have come along since, but it was Yale that set the earlier pace."

The game grew as more and more colleges took it up. In 1889 a new term was brought to the language—all-America. Camp and Casper Whitney, a writer, chose the best eleven players (one for each position) they had seen. The eleven came from Yale, Harvard, and Princeton so although the first all-America team didn't cover all of America it did create broad interest and become part of the history of football and the language of America.

On that first team was a guard from Yale named Walter (Pudge) Heffelfinger. Heffelfinger was the originator of many of the game's blocking techniques and he also initiated another important football tradition—the nickname.

Pudge Heffelfinger made the all-America team his last three seasons at Yale. The only reason he didn't make it in his first season was that it hadn't been invented yet.

Heffelfinger played and coached football for fifty years and he never forgot what he learned at Yale. Camp and Heffelfinger devised a lineman's stance that would give more leverage and better blocking position. When others told Heffelfinger that the practice wouldn't work in the more modern game, he said, "I didn't do it on muscle. I did it on method. I stood more or less erect, knees bent in a slight crouch, body leaning forward from the hips, legs spread three feet apart, left foot advanced. From a semi-standing stance, you can look the defense formation over, or size up the enemy grouping on attack. By watching the ball closely, you can detect the slightest flexing of the enemy center's hands—the tipoff that he's going to snap the ball—and thus time your charge."

Today we call that a key and linemen are still looking for that edge.

The college game grew and expanded westward and southward. As the nineteenth century drew to a close, players from colleges in the midwest began to appear on Camp's all-America teams. Then, in 1901 the balance of power shifted as Fielding Yost's team at Michigan ran up 501 points in 10 games and allowed none. The team deservedly was called "The Point-a-Minute" squad. In Pasadena, California the organizers of the Tournament of Roses thought that a football game would be a nice centerpiece to their annual New Year's Day event. Yost's Michigan team was invited out west to play the best team in California—Stanford University. Stanford was in its tenth season of football but already it had a rich tradition. Its first coach was none other than Walter Camp. One of Camp's successors was none other than Fielding Yost. But on this holiday, Yost was guiding Michigan and the Wolverines kept their perfect record intact as they trounced Stanford, 49-0. The Michigan team ran off 142 plays (about 60 a game is the average now) and gained 1,463 yards. There was no passing. All of that came on running plays.

The organizers of the Tournament of Roses found that chariot races and motorcycle races were more competitive and better served to highlight their big show. The Rose Bowl game was not played again until 1916.

Football faced its most serious test in 1905 as the first president who talked football, Theodore Roosevelt, demanded that the game's dangerous tactics be curbed. Eighteen players had died in the 1905 season and Roosevelt, who was almost evangelical on the subject of physical fitness, called Walter Camp and other coaches to the White House and said enough was enough. Restructure the game or lose it.

"Brutality and foul play," the President said, "should receive the same summary punishment given to a man who cheats at cards."

The coaches formed a rules committee and made changes. They made the game safer, to be sure, but the most significant change in the rules to come out of that meeting in January 1906 was the forward pass. The world of football would never be the same. John W. Heisman had tried to foster the use of the forward pass with his teams at Auburn in the 1890s. But passing the ball was not specifically allowed under the rules of the day so Heisman (for whom the Heisman Trophy is named) had to wait. And while he waited he taught his players the value of holding on to the ball.

"What is this?" he would ask his team at their first meeting each season. He was holding a football and gave his own answer. "A prolate spheroid—that is, an elongated sphere—in which the outer leather casing is drawn tightly over a somewhat small rubber tubing. Better to have died as a small boy than to fumble this football."

That rules committee not only saved the game but reaffirmed a football tradition of tinkering constantly with the rules in an effort to keep offense and defense in balance while focusing a keen eye on safety.

As the game developed so did great players. The finest offensive player of the game appeared on the college scene just a year after the rules changes opened up the sport. His name was Jim Thorpe, a Sac and Fox Indian who played at the Carlisle Institute, a trade school for Indians. Thorpe did it all. He passed the ball, kicked it 80 yards or more, tackled with strength and purpose, blocked like a man much larger. But what he did best was run. He could run over or around would-be tacklers. He played two years for Carlisle, left to play semipro baseball, and then returned for two more years at Carlisle. An eyewitness to Carlisle's victory over Army in 1912 was impressed.

"He simply ran wild, while the Cadets tried in vain to stop his progress. It was like trying to clutch a shadow."

At the time Thorpe was astonishing the Eastern football establishment, a Catholic University in Indiana was establishing a team in the Midwest. With Gus Dorais at quarterback and a man named Knute Rockne at end, the Irish were perfecting the forward pass. When Notre Dame came east in 1913 to play Army, Dorais and Rockne stunned the Cadets with their passing proficiency. This was not the invention of the forward pass, but it was a kind of coming out party for the play. Notre Dame won, 35-13.

"It was like shooting fish in a barrel." Dorais said years later.

Where was professional football through all of this? In effect nowhere. Oh, some players did get paid for playing once they had graduated from college. It is said that Pudge Heffelfinger got $500 for playing a game in 1892. But Heff was the exception and every attempt to start professional teams and professional leagues had failed. There was never enough interest. When a newspaper in Masillon, Ohio, revealed that a 1906 professional game between Masillon and Canton had been fixed, further interest on a professional level almost disappeared.

But the promoters kept trying. When Jim Thorpe decided to play professional football along with several of his teammates at Carlisle, the game started to inch forward. Then, in September, 1920 at a meeting of several promoters of pro teams at an automobile showroom in Canton, Ohio, the American Football Association was formed. This was the forerunner of the National Foodball League. The president (actually an honorary title) was Jim Thorpe.

Eleven clubs put up $100 apiece to form the league. "This was propaganda designed to give our new organization a facade of financial stability," said George Halas, who was present at the creation. "No money changed hands."

It does now. Pro football franchises have been sold for more than $50 million; the television networks pay the NFL around $400 million a year to broadcast its games; a quarterback named Steve Young has a contract with the new United States Football League that will be worth about $40 million over its 40-year term.

Although the NFL was formed in 1920, college football remained vastly more important and more popular for years to come.

"Outlined against the blue-gray October sky, the Four Horsemen rode again. In dramatic lore they were known as famine, pestilence, destruction, and death. These are only aliases. Their real names are Stuhldreher, Miller, Crowley, and Layden." Thus began a game report written in October, 1924 by Grantland Rice, the leading sportswriter of the day. And thus began his chronicle of Notre Dame's most famous group of players. That 13-7 victory over Army in New York helped the Irish on their way to an unbeaten season. The backfield of Harry Stuhldreher, Don Miller, Jim Crowley, and Elmer Layden had played together for three seasons and by this time they were so good that they impressed even so experienced an observer as Rice. A slick Notre Dame publicist read Rice's account, and back home in Indiana, put the players on horseback for a photograph. Newspapers around the country printed it and to this day, the Four Horsemen of Notre Dame remain football's most famous unit.

Over football's years it has always been the custom to hang a nickname on a team or part of a team. Notre Dame's Four Horsemen might not have been successful were it not for the Seven Mules blocking for them.

Football has had the Vow Boys (Stanford), the Seven Blocks of Granite (Fordham), the Touchdown Twins (Army), and dozens of others. In most recent years pro football has continued the pattern of nicknaming teams or units. There have been the Monsters of the Midway (Chicago Bears), the Doomsday Defense (Dallas Cowboys), the Purple People Eaters (Minnesota Vikings), the New York Sack Exchange (New York Jets), and the Smurfs, the Fun Bunch, and the Hogs (all Washington Redskins).

There have been others. There will be more. Football has a tendency to develop personnae of groups rather than individuals. It is the ultimate team game. Jim Brown would have gained very few yards if it weren't for his blockers; Lawrence Taylor couldn't cause his freelance wreckage if other Giant defenders weren't occupying their opponents; Joe Namath's bullet passes would have lost their zing without sure-fingered receivers. There are eleven men on the field and more than forty on a team. They all are important.

In the sport at the college level, virtually every school has one game that means more than all others. There is The Game (Harvard vs. Yale). On the west coast there is The Big Game (Stanford vs. California). And over the years these and other traditional rivalries have sustained their importance. In The Big Game of 1982, Stanford was leading, 20-19, when it kicked off to California just before the final gun sounded. Kevin Moen caught the kickoff and lateraled to Richard Rodgers. He ran about 10 yards and lateraled to Dwight Garner, who ran about 20 yards. By now the gun had sounded and fans and Stanford's band had run onto the field, thinking the game was over. But it was not. Garner lateraled the ball to Marriet Ford who quickly lateraled it back to Moen. He zig-zagged his way through the Stanford players, the fans, and the band into the end zone for a 25-20 victory. The writer Roy Blount said that he thought Stanford's defense was "a little weak in the woodwinds."

But it was no joke to Stanford's coach Paul Wiggin. The 1983 season was a bad one for Stanford and he believed much of it stemmed from that play.

"The things that can happen in four seconds." Wiggin said. "That play changed everything. If we had won, we'd have come into this season with momentum. I remember walking off the field and telling my wife, 'The ramifications of this are far beyond what you realize now.'"

Wiggin was fired.

If football has enriched our language with its lively terms, its colorful nicknames, and the pithy words of its story-tellers, some fans' passions have stopped other people from talking.

There is the story of the man who was watching his fourth football game of the weekend when his wife stepped in front of the television and said, "You love football more than me."

He gently pushed her aside, stared back at the set and said, "Yes dear, but I love you more than basketball."

LEXICON

Alley oop

n: a pass play made famous by Y.A. Tittle and R.C. Owens of the San Francisco 49ers in the late 1950s. The play took advantage of Owens's remarkable leaping ability. Tittle would throw a pass toward the end zone, higher than the outstretched arms of all players save one—R.C. Owens.

all the lights aren't on

adj. phrase: what one player says about another, the one who will never be confused with a rocket scientist.

animal

n: a player who loves to get physical and will do so during a play or without regard for the referee's whistle, which is supposed to stop play.

Matt Millen

at the door

prep. phrase: the team is near the goal line and about to score. Also has been used by Bum Phillips to describe how close a team can come to winning a Super Bowl. After his Houston Oiler team of 1979 had lost the American Football Conference championship game

(at the door cont'd)
for the second straight year he said, "Last year we knocked at the door. This year we kicked at the door, and next year we're gonna knock the damn door down." Unfortunately for Phillips the Oilers huffed and puffed and kicked but they couldn't knock the door down. He was fired.

Bum Phillips

audible

v: to signal a change in the play after it has been called in the huddle but before the ball has been snapped. A quarterback, seeking to counter the defensive formation the opponents are in, barks out a series of commands that tells his team to execute a play different from the one he has just chosen in the huddle. The audible might be geared to a color code. By changing the first word of the count before the ball is snapped, the quarterback tells his teammates that the play has been changed and what it has been changed to.

Blistering

part: speed so fast that the friction of that player's

(blistering cont'd)

feet on the turf would raise blisters on the feet of a mere mortal player.

Nolan Cromwell

blitz

v: to have a defensive player (one who ordinarily does not charge) charge at the quarterback. Usually it is a safety. Since he plays farther behind the line than any other defender, he has a head of steam up by the time he reaches the quarterback. If the play is unexpected and no blockers pick up the charging safety, a big yardage loss or even a fumble may result. On the other hand, if the blitzer is blocked, the quarterback can pass to the man the safety was supposed to cover and a large gain may be the result.

blue-chipper

n: a top recruit for a college football team. Also a scout's term for the top player or players for an upcoming opponent.

bomb

n: a long pass completion, often for a touchdown. Another of those terms where football imitates war (although some might say that it is war that imitates football).

bookends

n: two outside linemen (tackles on offense, ends on defense) who each play so well that they hold the rest of the line together.

bootleg

n: a running play designed for the quarterback. He takes the snap, fakes giving the ball to a running back, and then holds the ball alongside his leg. He scampers in the opposite direction from the running teammate to whom he has faked giving the ball.

breakaway back

n: a runner who combines speed, deception, and strength to elude the grasp of a defender. In the 1950s Jon Arnett and Ollie Matson gave the Los Angeles Rams two of football's best breakaway backs.

Among the "Seven Blocks of Granite" were (l. to r.) Vince Lombardi, Alex Wojciechowicz, Nat Pierce and Leo Paquin.

brick wall

n: a player (or players) who cannot be moved aside or run over. An immovable force that can resist virtually any object. In football's early days one of the best known "brick walls" was the unit called the "Seven Blocks of Granite" at Fordham University. These players—Vince Lombardi (who gained more fame many years later as the great coach of the Green Bay Packers), Johnny Druze, Al Babartsky, Alex Wojciechowicz, Nat Pierce, Ed Franco, and Leo Paquin—helped make Fordham one of the ruling powers in the world of college football in the mid 30s.

bring in the chains

v: to stop play and have the sideline officials walk in with the chains (exactly 10 yards long) to see if the offensive team has advanced the ball the 10 yards needed for a first down.

broken-field runner

n: a runner who is at his best when he continually has to sidestep defenders on his way downfield. Hugh McElhenny of the San Francisco 49ers in the 1950s got the nickname of "King" because there was no one better at darting and slipping through a field of defending players.

broken play

n: a play that doesn't go exactly as planned. For whatever reason—a defender got in the way or an offensive player didn't remember what play was called—the quarterback is forced to improvise, sometimes with disastrous results. A player causing too many broken plays because of his lack of concentration and execution is sure to be looking for employment elsewhere.

bull

n: a big, strong, and fast running back.

Bert Jones

bullet pass

n: a ball thrown very hard and accurately, comparable to the trajectory of a rifle shot.

bump and run

v: to play up close to the man being guarded in order to try to stop him or slow him down by bumping into him as he comes across the line. The run comes after the bump when the receiver has been slowed and the defensive back runs alongside him. For

(bump and run cont'd)

many years, Pat Fischer was considered among the finest defensive backs in pro football because he was so proficient at bumping and running. His theory was that if he bumped you and you both fell, he could get up faster than you could, effectively keeping you out of the play. Alas, the rulesmakers of the NFL realized that this technique kept receivers from getting free and resulted in too many low scoring games. The rules were changed to cut down on bumping and running. The types of defensive backs who played like Pat Fischer eventually were bumped and run right out of pro football.

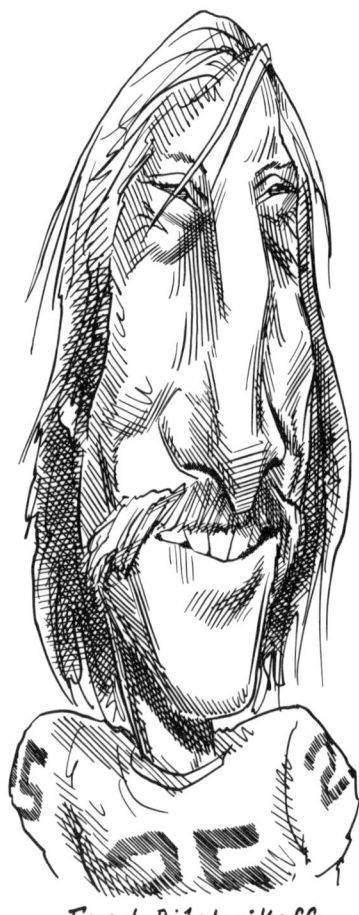

Fred Biletnikoff buttonhook-man

burner

n: a wide receiver whose speed is best for the first few yards beyond the line of scrimmage. After that he becomes a good—but not especially dangerous—receiver.

buttonhook

n: a pass route run by a receiver, often one without outstanding speed. In this pattern the receiver will run downfield about 15 yards, spin around and make a U-turn back toward the quarterback. If drawn on a sheet of paper or a locker-room blackboard, the pattern closely resembles a hook used for pulling buttons through buttonholes on some old-fashioned shoes.

Cadence

n: the rhythm of a quarterback's count and call as the ball is about to be snapped. By altering his cadence, the quarterback can throw the defenders off stride as they try to guess at what point the play actually will begin. Also by altering his cadence, a signal-caller might be indicating to his team a slight variation in the play.

Ken Riley

catlike

n: a term of quickness (not necessarily a term of endearment) applied to a defensive back whose moves have a feline grace and quality to them.

center

n: the man who begins the action. When the play is about to start he leans over the ball, places his hand or hands on it and snaps it back between his legs to the quarterback on the prearranged signal.

v: to snap the ball through your legs toward the quarterback.

Mick Tingelhoff

chip shot

n: an easy field goal attempt. One which should be about as makeable for the place-kicker as a shot of about 80 yards to the green should be for the professional golfer. Of course, there are no sure things.

chuck

v: to ward off an opponent by hitting him with a quick motion of the arms followed by the return of the arms to a flexed non-contact position. This maneuver, when observed by the officials, results in a penalty.

circus catch

n: a catch made by a receiver downfield that seemed to be impossible—only good hands, an acrobat's skill, and a superb effort by the receiver makes the catch possible.

Lynn Swann

clipping

part: running or diving into the back of an opponent, or throwing one's body across the back of the leg or legs of an opponent other than the ball carrier. A dangerous and illegal maneuver but one that often cannot be avoided. In the rapidly changing flow of a football play, the man facing you at the moment you are about to block him may turn his back

(clipping cont'd)
to you at the time you actually block him. But no excuses—
if you're caught, your team pays the penalty.

clothesline tackle

n: the stopping of a ball carrier by thrusting your arm sideways at him as he runs toward you. Usually the arm is thrust out so the runner's Adam's apple makes first contact with the arm. It's kind of like running through a back alley and getting caught in the neck by the rope holding Mrs. O'Brien's wet wash.

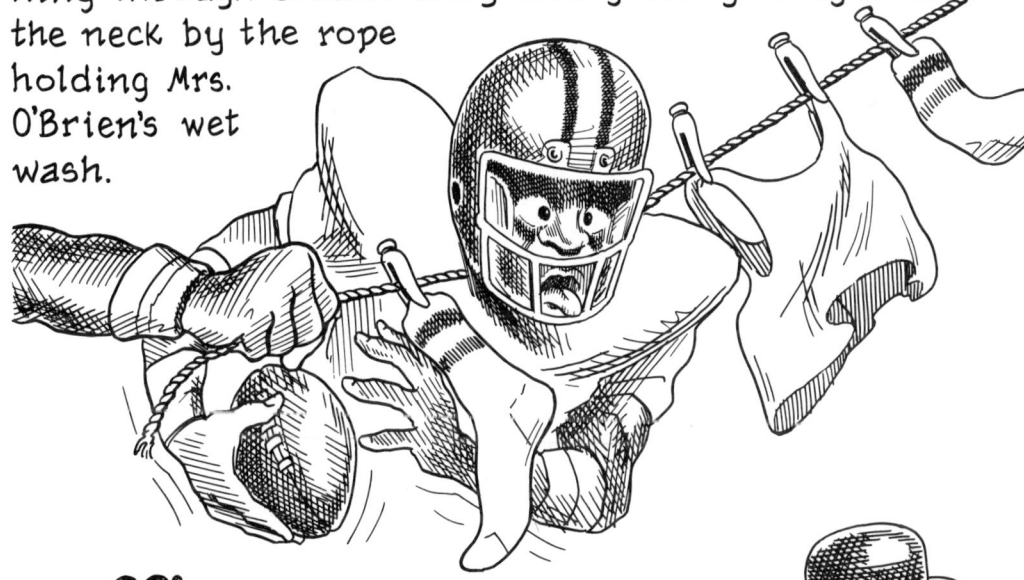

coffin corner

n: the corners of the field near your own end zone. When one team is punting within the 50-yard line, the kicker often will try to kick the ball so it goes out of bounds as close to the goal line as possible, or goes dead inbounds in those corners. If the kicker executes properly, he may have killed off your chances of moving the ball forward and scoring.

Ray Guy

containment

n: the act of holding off your opponent on the line. Not really dominating him, just keeping him from making a big play.

co-op blocking

part: after the ball is snapped, two offensive lineman charging toward one defensive lineman to keep him out of the play. To further confound the defender, the blocker on the outside will slide around and try to block a linebacker.

Joe Jacoby and Russ Grimm

cornerback

n: this man is responsible for preventing receptions or tackling the receivers on the offensive team. The receivers have two advantages — incredible speed and knowledge of where the play is supposed to go. But the cornerback is usually one of the best athletes on the team for he must be fast and have outstanding reflexes. He must be able to withstand stress because if his man beats him, it usually results in a touchdown. Everson Walls of the Dallas Cowboys, one of the best cornerbacks, offered

Everson Walls

(cornerback cont'd)
these words during the 1983 season in an interview in *Pro Magazine,* "Playing the corner is like playing tag on a tightrope. You're out there in the open and the whole world is watching. There are no small mistakes, only giant ones. One slip and it's goodbye."

counter play

n: a running play in which the action and movement of the offensive line and the quarterback are in one direction (to the right, say) while the ball is handed to a running back heading the opposite way.

crackback block

n: an illegal (and very dangerous) blocking technique in which a receiver heads down field as if he were involved in a pass play. But he cuts (or cracks) back toward the line of scrimmage and blocks at the backs of the knees of a linebacker or defensive lineman.

crawling

part: an attempt (one that is penalized if detected) by a player to advance the ball after he actually has been tackled and the play is dead. This maneuver is particularly effective in a situation where the large number of players in a pileup

(crawling cont'd)
blocks the officials' view.

cut back

v: to change directions very suddenly trying to avoid a tackler.

Delay

v: to hold your position at the line of scrimmage for a second or two after the ball is snapped, hoping to decoy your defender into thinking you are not involved in the play. After counting off a second or two, you head downfield with a jump on the defender.

depth chart

n: an easy reference chart for coaches, players, and fans that lists the starters for a team and the players held in reserve. Most depth charts go three deep at each position with some players holding down the role of backup at several positions.

dive play

n: a straight-ahead, no-deception running play in which the ball carrier heads right for the line of scrimmage and tries to dive over the blockers and tacklers or

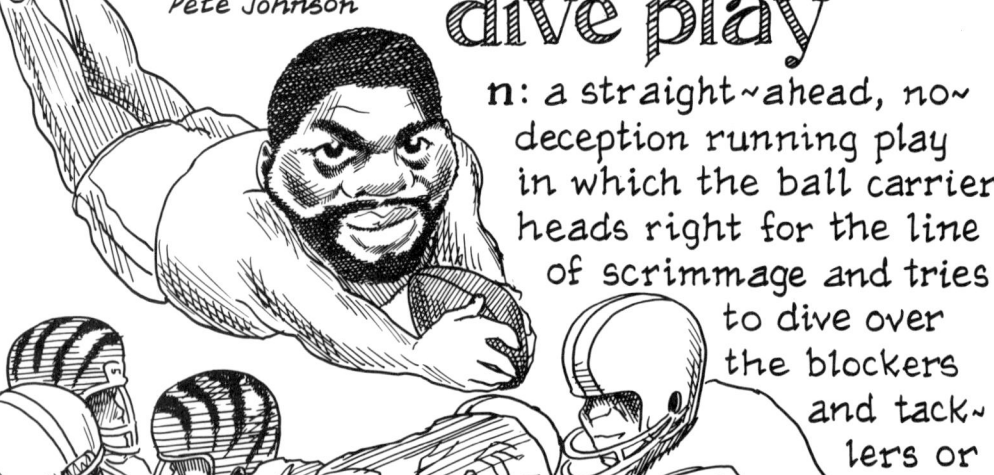
Pete Johnson

(dive play cont'd) through them in an attempt to gain short, tough yardage.

Anthony Munoz

domination block

n: a block by an offensive lineman that is so effective that the man he is blocking is pinned to the ground and has no chance of getting involved in the play.

don't hit him, he's dead

inter: a phrase used by a referee to get the defensive players to stop from unnecessarily "hitting" the quarterback. To protect the quarterback, the referee shouts this to let the defensive linemen know that the quarterback has released his pass and is no longer a legal target.

down

n: any play by the team in possession of the ball. A team has four downs to advance the ball 10 yards. If they are not successful, the opponents take over and their offense gets a crack at moving 10 yards or more in four downs.

down and out

n: a pass route in which the receiver runs down the field and then cuts out toward the sideline trying to get away from the defensive back. A down and in is a play in which the receiver heads downfield and makes his cut inside.

draft

n: one of the biggest days of the year in pro football. Held in the spring, it is the time the teams choose players from the best of that year's college seniors. On draft day, invariably, hope is high as the team lists all the can't miss prospects it has chosen. The way it works basically is this: the team with the worst record the previous season chooses first and then choices continue through the league until each team has, in inverse order to the standing, picked a player. The theory is that the weaker teams can get stronger by choosing each season's best available players. This, of course, does not always happen as attested by the New York Giants' continued failures and the Los Angeles Raiders' continued success.

draw play

n: a running play in which the quarterback drops back with the ball as if he is about to pass. One of the running backs stands his ground as if he is going to block for

(draw play cont'd)
the quarterback. But as the quarterback goes by the running back he slides the ball into the hands of the runner, who takes off. For the play to work, offensive linemen initially have to block as if the play is a pass and the defense must have visualized the play as a pass and have started toward the quarterback just as the runner headed downfield.

drop back

v: a quarterback's move. To back pedal away from the line of scrimmage after taking the snap from the center. A classic quarterback will drop back seven steps, set up straight, plant his back foot, scan the field looking for a receiver and hope that his blockers hold the defense off long enough to deliver the pass.

Bart Starr

drop kick

n: an antiquated form of kicking for points in which the ball was snapped directly to the kicker who let it fall to the ground in a controlled manner and kicked it towards the uprights just as it hit the ground. Drop kicks became outdated because the football is less round and there is no guarantee that the ball won't take a bad bounce when it is dropped.

dump off

v: to throw a pass to a receiver close by who was not the prime target. The quarterback dumps the ball

(dump off cont'd)

off when his receivers are covered downfield or he is under pressure from defensive players.

Eat nails

v: to be so tough that your regular breakfast is supposed to come from a barrel at the hardware store. No one was quite sure what size nail Dick Butkus ate while he was with the Chicago Bears terrorizing running backs and quarterbacks.

eat the ball

v: what a quarterback does when he is tackled after dropping back to pass, failing to find an open receiver, and being unable to run. In this case, digestion is the better part of valor for a misguided pass could result in an interception.

encroachment

n: a penalty called when a player enters the neu-

(encroachment cont'd)
tral zone between the offensive line and the defensive line or makes contact with an opponent before the ball is snapped

end around

n: a running play in which a wide receiver leaves his position on the line of scrimmage, runs toward the quarterback, takes the handoff, and continues running around the other end. For this play to work, two things are needed—surprise and the outstanding speed of the wide receiver. On the negative side is the fact that the play develops deep in the offensive team's backfield and if a defender is on the spot, a big loss is the result.

end-over-end

adj: how a punted ball travels when it is spinning in the air from one point of the ball to the other.

Face mask

n: the cage-like front of a player's helmet. At times the mask is grabbed by an opponent to get leverage, an illegal maneuver that sometimes results in an injury and often results in a penalty.

fair catch

n: the reception of a kicked ball when the opposing

(fair catch cont'd)

players are not allowed to tackle the receiver. This is signaled by his raising one hand above his head and waving it from side to side.

field goal

n: a score that counts three points for kicking the ball over the crossbar and between the goal posts.

Jan Stenerud

field position

n: where a team has possession of the ball. This often determines the types of offensive plays a team can make. Near its own goal line (bad field position), many coaches don't like to pass, fearing an interception.

Dick Vermeil

films

n: movies of each team's game. Coaches are so dedicated to these movies that they spend many hours each week viewing them in front of projectors. And some will not analyze their games with interviewers until they've seen the films.

find the seam

v: to discover the defense's area of greatest vulnerability. In certain defenses a (find the seam cont'd) player is responsible for an area, a teammate is responsible for the bordering area. Where these sectors meet, is the "seam." If a quarterback locates his receiver in that spot, there usually is a completion.

Dwight Clark and Joe Montana seam-finders

fire out

v: to move off the offensive line quickly and powerfully as the ball is snapped.

flag

n: the penalty marker (usually a yellow kerchief) used by officials.

flag football

n: a form of the game often played in college intramurals. Each player eligible to score wears flag-like streamers attached to his belt. No tackling is allowed in this game. To stop a runner or receiver you must pull off one of those streamers.

flanker

n: a back who is positioned away from the rest of the backfield and normally is a pass receiver. This position is now referred to as wide receiver.

flare out

v: to roll out of the backfield in order to catch a pass.

flat

n: the area directly to the left or right of the line of scrimmage in an offensive formation.

flea flicker

n: a razzle-dazzle play in which the quarterback takes the snap from the center, drops back as if to pass, and instead tosses a lateral pass to a teammate who feigns advancing the ball. Then that player tosses another lateral back to the quarterback. (All this is legal so long as none of these passes move the ball forward or are beyond the line of scrimmage) Now the quarterback has the ball back, hoping he has the defense thoroughly confused and that a receiver is wide open far downfield for a long gaining play. Sometimes this is the case, but the more people handling the ball the more chances for misplays. So the flea flicker is rarely seen in professional football or top level college football. The best place to see it may be a sandlot game in your local park. Watch for it there. You're sure to spot it.

Wes Chandler

flood the zone

v: to send more pass receivers into an area of the field than there are defenders.

fly pattern

n: a pass route in which the receiver comes off the line and just races or flies down the field, trying to leave all defenders behind.

flying wedge

n: an antiquated and now banned formation in which ten players would form a V-shape around the ball carrier, link arms and fend off tacklers. This often resulted in injury. Around the turn of the century there was an outcry against this and other dangerous tactics of power football. In 1905 President Theodore Roosevelt said that if the game wasn't tamed, he would ban football by presidential decree. By January 1906 a rules committee was formed that helped bring the sport out of the dark — and dangerous — age.

40

n: the classic distance (40 yards) in measuring how fast a player can run. The supposition is that rarely does a player have to make a run of more than 40 yards during a game.

forward fumble

n: a risky maneuver in which a tackled player drops the ball intentionally hoping that it will go out of bounds far enough ahead of him so as to pick up some extra yardage. The risk is that it won't go out of bounds and an opponent will recover the fumble.

Herschel Walker

free kick

n: the instance when a player is allowed to kick the

(free kick cont'd)

ball without interference from any opposing player. Free kicks usually come after a team gives up a safety.

free safety

n: the position in the defensive backfield that is often likened to the center fielder in baseball. The free safety is not responsible for any specific offensive player but he follows the play and responds to the direction it is going.

freeze

v: to stop a defender in his tracks by bringing an offensive player into his area. When the offensive player makes his move, he hopes to catch the frozen defender flatfooted.

front four

n: the line in defensive formations consisting of two tackles and two ends. Among the more well known

The "Sack Exchange"

(front four cont'd)

"Front Fours" were the Ram's Fearsome Foursome of Merlin Olsen, Deacon Jones, Lamar Lundy and Roosevelt Grier; the Steel Curtain from Pittsburgh of Mean Joe Greene, Dwight White, Ernie Holmes and L.C. Greenwood, and the Jets' Sack Exchange of Mark Gastineau, Marty Lyons, Abdul Salaam and Joe Klecko.

fullback

n: the offensive back stationed behind the quarterback, usually called on to get the tough yards on running plays.

Earl Campbell 34

fumble

v: to drop the ball.

Gamer

n: a guy who will play under any circumstances. Injury or illness never stops him and he can be depended on to perform as well as he can for as long as he can. Also used to connote a player who will save himself for the game by hardly putting out in practice. When Jean Fugett played for the Dallas Cowboys in the mid-70s his teammates called him a gamer, saying he would phone in his practices if he could.

game plan

n: the game strategy and the plays needed to make it work, as determined by the coaches before the start of play. Each team plots in advance what it will do depending on who the opponents are and what

(game plan cont'd)

their tendencies are. This scheme is known as the game plan.

gang tackle

v: to stop a ball carrier with more than one (many more than one) defender.

gap

n: an opening, either between two offensive or two defensive linemen. The defenders try to get through these openings to stop the ball carrier. The offense tries to get through to throw a downfield block.

get off the ball

v: to make a fast start off the offensive line once the ball has been put into play.

goal-line defense

n: the powerful opposition to a team "at the door." In these formations, the biggest and strongest players line up solidly to try to keep the offense out of the end zone.

go against the grain

v: to move opposite from the direction that almost everyone else is going.

go north and south

v: to run straight ahead without getting fancy. Simply an attempt to move the ball forward.

grind it out

v: to gain yardage in small amounts with a running or short passing game that moves the ball inexorably downfield.

John Hannah

guard

n: the lineman positioned beside the center. He has the most responsibility for blocking on running plays.

Halftime

n: the intermission between the second quarter and the third quarter in which the bands march on the field, the concessionaires sell in the stands, and the fans at home watch the taped TV highlights of games played in other cities.

hang time

n: the number of seconds a punt stays in the air. The greater the number of seconds, the easier it is for the punting team to get downfield and tackle the receiver.

hash marks

n: the inbounds line markers, spaced one yard apart, which fix the point where the ball is put in play.

head hunter

n: a rough player, usually a defensive player, who is looking to put his opponent out of the game each time he hits him. Sometimes those hits are within the rules, sometimes not.

hear footsteps

v: to be so aware of a defensive player about to hit you that you lose your concentration as you await the ball. You get this message usually when you're about to receive a pass with your back turned away from the defender.

Heisman Trophy

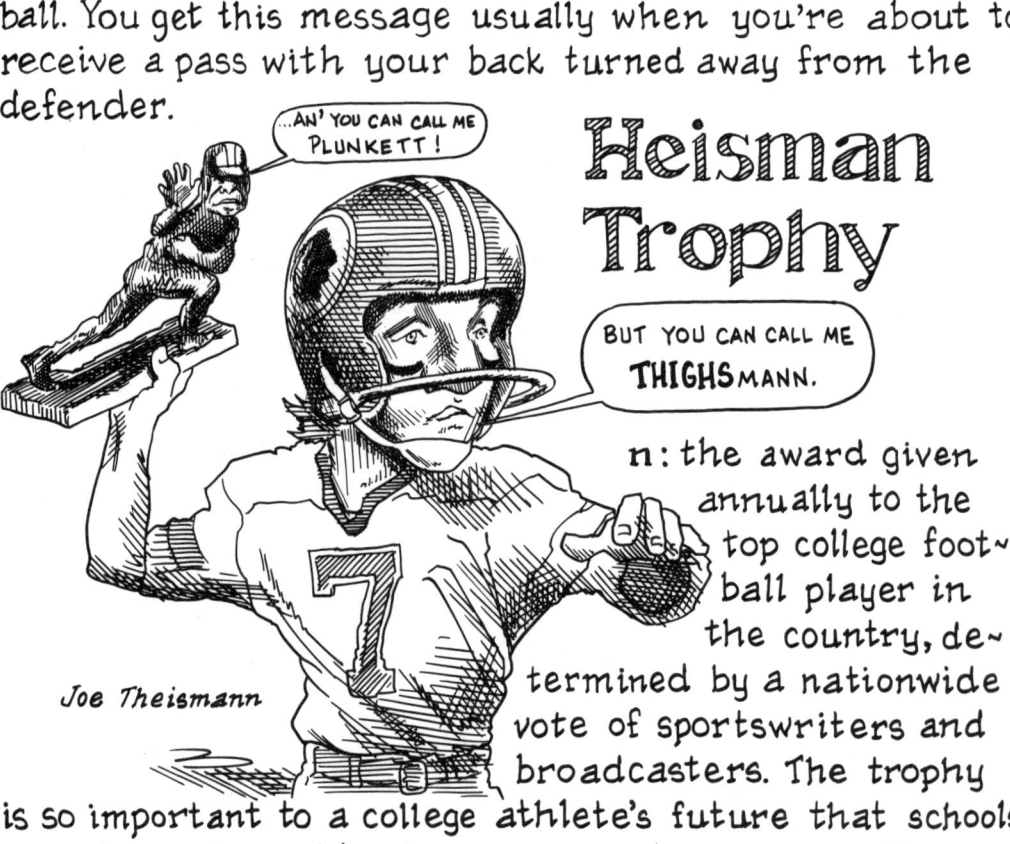

Joe Theismann

...AN' YOU CAN CALL ME PLUNKETT!

BUT YOU CAN CALL ME THIGHSMANN.

n: the award given annually to the top college football player in the country, determined by a nationwide vote of sportswriters and broadcasters. The trophy is so important to a college athlete's future that schools mount massive publicity campaigns to get more attention

(Heisman Trophy cont'd)
for a star athlete. When Joe Theismann was an undergraduate at Notre Dame, he was convinced that changing the pronunciation of his name from THEES-man, as his family had always pronounced it, to THIGHS-man, to rhyme with HIGHS-man would help his chances. Theismann continues to use the new pronunciation although in his senior year he finished second to Jim Plunkett of Stanford in the voting for the 1970 trophy.

hightops

John Unitas

n: the old-fashioned black over-the-ankle leather shoes once worn by virtually all football players. As time went by, lowcut shoes became the norm so that top quarterbacks Y.A. Tittle of the Giants and Johnny Unitas of the Colts became even more conspicuous in their latter years because they stuck with the high shoes.

hitch

n: a quick sprint downfield by a receiver followed by a quick turn back toward the quarterback to catch a pass.

hold and release

v: to stay at the line of scrimmage momentarily after the ball is snapped and then to run downfield on a pass pattern. This is done to decoy the defensive player into thinking the receiver is not part of the play.

holding

part: the penalty for using the hands illegally to impede the progress of an opponent. It is against the rules for an offensive player to use his hands to impede a defender or for a defensive player to use them to tackle any offensive player other than the one with the ball.

hot dog

n: a player who uses extravagant movements to show up an opponent. In recent years the main hot dog maneuver has been the end zone dance of players who have scored a touchdown. Mark Gastineau of the Jets has brought the hot dog to the defense with his "Sack Dance," done each time he tackles a quarterback. Billy (White Shoes) Johnson, a graduate of tiny Widener College, used his end zone dances after touchdowns to gain notoriety. This and the fact that he scored many touchdowns helped establish his career. The NFL is attempting to legislate the hot dog out of existence and passed a rule in the spring of 1984 barring dancing on the field.

Billy Johnson

huddle

n: the meeting of the minds before each play. On offense the quarterback assembles his team behind the line of scrimmage to tell them what the next play will be. On defense, one player tells his teammates what he thinks the next play might be and calls a defensive formation.

Iceman

Bud Grant

n: a player or coach who seems to be unaffected by the cold.

I formation

n: an offensive arrangement in which the two running backs line up single file directly behind the quarterback, thus forming the letter "I" in the backfield. This is a good formation to showcase one outstanding runner, the deep back in the "I." He has more room to pick up speed while moving toward the line, more time to find the open areas, and more blockers moving along with the front back in the "I" ready to cut down, or deflect a defender or two.

Tony Dorsett

impact player

n: a running back who, because of his speed and offensive moves, suddenly can change the course of a game. He rarely is a starter but is inserted to give a team a quick boost.

in the trenches

prep. phrase: where the action is at the moment the ball is snapped. The hand-to-hand battles that

(in the trenches cont'd)

go on between offensive and defensive lineman has been compared to the hand-to-hand combat seen in Europe in World War I.

intentional grounding

adj. phrase: a penalty called on a quarterback who, as he is about to be tackled, throws the ball into an area where there is no eligible receiver near enough to catch it. The quarterback grounds the ball, realizing that it's better to lose just a down because of an incomplete pass than to lose a down and yardage by being tackled far behind the line of scrimmage. But if the referee determines there was no chance of the quarterback's completing the pass, a penalty is assessed.

interception

n: a pass caught by a defensive player instead of the intended receiver.

interference

n: the penalty for impeding a player (either on offense or defense) who is trying to catch a pass.

Jam

v: to stop a receiver legally as he tries to come off the line of scrimmage and run his pass pattern.

jump pass

n: a ball thrown by a quarterback as he leaps into the air. The quarterback sacrifices the power he normally would have if he kept his feet planted but he gains some vision over charging, arm-waving defensive linemen.

Keys

n: the things that indicate where a play is heading. By viewing game films and scouting the opponents, you can often tell by certain movements what is about to happen. (The way an offensive lineman assumes his stance might be a key to a run or pass play. The way the defensive backs are set might tip off a blitz.) Of course, a team can make a change that makes those keys meaningless.

Joe Namath

knee

n: the part of the anatomy that is most vulnerable for a football player. To have a knee tells simply that your knee has been injured. It doesn't say exactly how but

(knee cont'd)
it does say that you have trouble.

Lateral

n: a pass thrown sideways or backwards from one player to another. When the ball is carried beyond the line of scrimmage, it is against the rules to pass the ball toward the opponent's goal line.

limpoffs

n: a category that never shows up in the official statistics. One player may try to put an opponent out of commission, to have him "limp off" the field. The number of players who sustain such injuries defines this brutal statistic.

linebacker

n: the defensive position behind the line of scrimmage and in front of the secondary. Because of the way defenses are set up, these players make the majority of tackles. Often a team's best athlete is a linebacker because of his speed, agility, and strength.

Lawrence Taylor

look in

n: a play in which the receiver comes off the line of scrimmage, runs diagonally down and across the field and looks over his shoulder to catch a quick pass.

look off

v: to fake a defender into moving in the wrong direction by looking one way while throwing a pass the other.

looping

part: a defensive trick in which one lineman will circle around his teammate and charge at the offensive line from another angle, hoping to confuse the offense and muddle its blocking assignments.

Mack truck

n: a tough, practically unmoveable player, usually one on defense.

manster

n: a player who is so strong and so tough and so hard for an opponent to deal with that he is thought to be half man and half monster.

Randy White

man to man

n: a pass defense in which each back is responsible for one player and must stick with him wherever he goes.

meat grinder

n: the area of an opponent's greatest resistance. The offensive line of the Washington Redskins, the linebacking crew of the Giants, the defensive backfield of the Los Angeles Raiders have been known to grind up an opponent or two.

messenger

Paul Brown

n: a player responsible for bringing in the play called from the sidelines. When Paul Brown was coaching the Cleveland Browns in the mid-50s he had a messenger guard system. There were two offensive linemen approximately of equal ability who would substitute for each other on alternate plays, rushing to the huddle to tell the quarterback what play Coach Brown wanted called.

misdirection

n: a play in which most of the offensive linemen and the quarterback head one way, while the running back who has taken the ball goes another.

momentum

n: things going your way. A most important element of a football game. There is nothing tangible about this but you can sense it either on the field or in the stands. When a team has everything going its way it gathers momentum both on offense or defense, like an avalanche rushing down the mountainside with no force able to stop it.

Monday morning quarterback

n: someone who is an expert at second-guessing. He uses 20-20 hindsight to tell a football team on Monday what it should have done on Sunday.

monster back

n: a defensive player who has no set position but lines himself up in the spot where he expects the play to develop and where he feels he is needed.

move the pile

v: to push the defense back and get the better of the movement at the line of scrimmage. Doug English of the Detroit Lions spent a tough afternoon playing against Mike Baab, the Cleveland Browns' center,

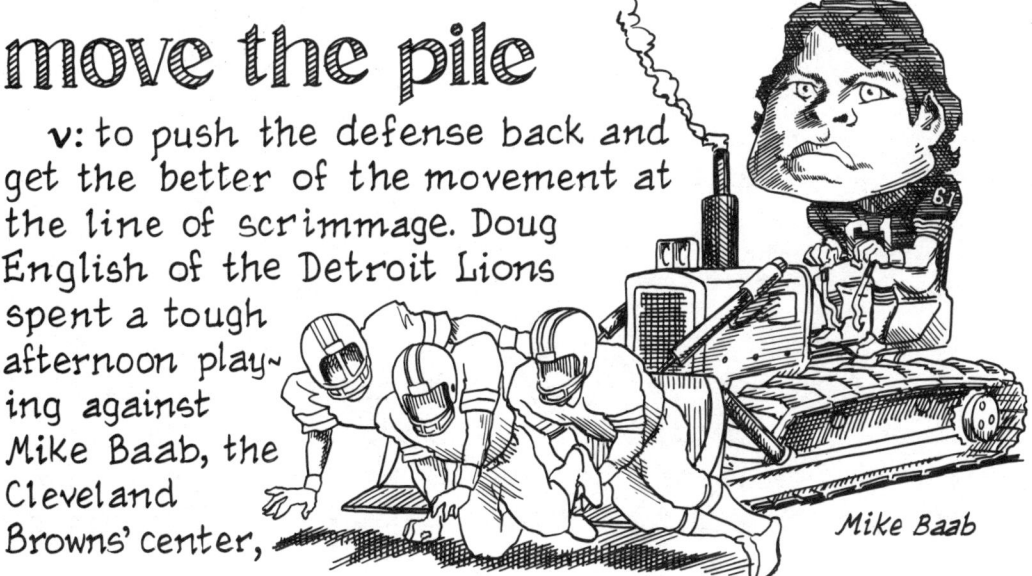

Mike Baab

(move the pile cont'd)

and said, "He moves the pile. 'e's as strong as nine acres of onions."

muff

v: to touch a loose ball (usually after a kick) in an unsuccessful attempt to gain possession.

multiple set

n: an offense that never looks the same way twice. It can have two backs running out of the "I"; it can have the quarterback alone behind the center with all the other backs moving out as pass receivers; it can have the tight end moving into the backfield. At times, it can combine all those elements—and more.

Nickel defense

n: a formation used in defending against an almost certain pass. A fifth defensive back—the nickle—is inserted to better cover the extra pass receivers. If a sixth defensive back is used, the formation, in keeping with the monetary nomenclature, is called the dime.

no shows

n: the number of fans who buy tickets for a game and then do not attend. This became an added statistic in pro football when the rule covering television blackouts of local events was changed in 1973. Before that, the theory went, fans went to the game

(no shows cont'd)
no matter what the weather because they could not see it on TV. Now, a soldout game is televised in the home market and if game day weather isn't good, many choose to watch from the comfort of their living room.

A "no show"

nose tackle

n: the position in the middle of a three-man defensive line, directly across from the nose of the offensive center. Because a three-man line is so outnumbered, the middle man usually has two or three offensive linemen to deal with and gets a lot of punishment.

nutcracker

n: a training camp drill designed to promote toughness. One player is usually squared off against two others who bounce him from one to the other. The lone player is attempting to get by, the duo is trying to stop him.

Offsides

n: a penalty resulting when any part of a player's body is into the neutral zone between the defensive line and the offensive line as the ball is snapped.

off-tackle

n: a running play in which the ball carrier runs into the line just outside an offensive tackle.

one-back offense

n: an offensive formation in which only one running back lines up behind the quarterback. Also called the Ace. It was devised by Joe Gibbs when he was the offensive coordinator of the San Diego Chargers and made popular by him as the head coach of the Washington Redskins. Gibbs worked it out in the late 70s when the defensive formations began to use four linebackers and three linemen. The second back had his spot taken by an extra tight end to improve the blocking. "If some 6-foot-4-inch, 225-pound linebacker, was going to blitz," Gibbs told Michael Janofsky of The New York Times, "I want a 6-foot-4-inch, 225-pound tight end blocking him."

John Riggins

onside kick

n: a short kickoff.

(onside kick cont'd)

Once a kickoff has traveled 10 yards, it is a free ball and the team that covers it gets possession. A team will try this type of kick if it is trailing and has just scored. By having the ball travel the required 10 yards but not much farther, the kicking team has a chance to recover the ball as it is bouncing around freely.

option

n: a play in which the quarterback keeps the ball and runs behind the line with the choice of either passing or trying to run with the ball beyond the line of scrimmage.

Doug English, penetrating.

Penetration

n: the act of getting into an opponent's territory, either into the defensive zone when you have the ball or into the opposition's offensive backfield when you don't.

piling on

n: a penalty called when, after the whistle has blown to halt the play, a defensive player jumps on the mass of bodies already on top of the ball carrier.

pinching

part: having two defensive linemen charge from each side of one blocker and catch him between them.

pit

n: yet another term for the area where offensive line crashes into the defensive line after the ball has been snapped. The action sometimes resembles animals trying to claw one another.

pitchout

n: an underhanded toss usually from the quarterback to a running back who is moving toward the sidelines. This helps get the ball to a runner who is already in motion and has built up momentum.

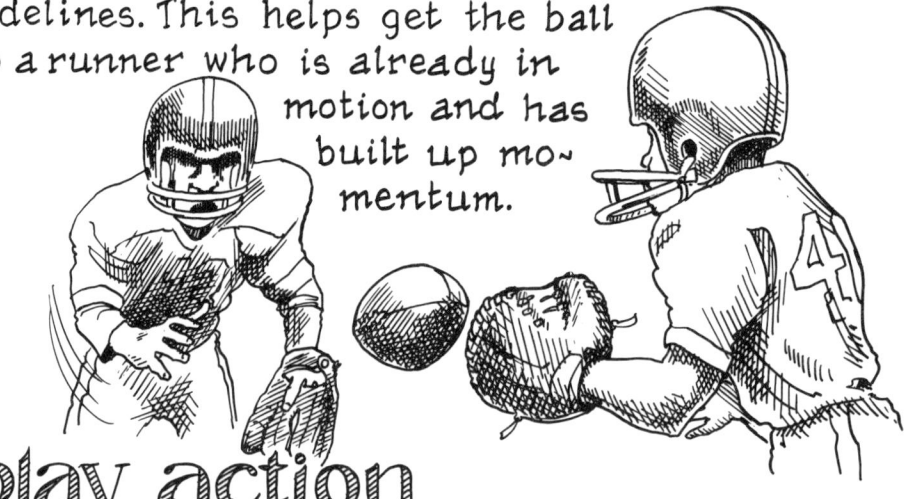

play action

n: an offensive play in which the quarterback fakes a handoff to a running back hoping to get the

(play action cont'd)
defense to react to a run. Then he passes.

playbook

n: the large volume each team prepares for its players that describes each one of the team's plays. The Washington Redskins are said to have 500 plays in their playbook.

play on a short field

v: to have the ball in good position, that is with relatively few yards to go to the goal line.

plug a hole

v: to fill an opening in the line created by the offense, one in which a defender has previously been knocked aside, thereby stopping the ball-carrier.

pocket

n: the protective wall formed by the offensive linemen trying to block for the quarterback who has retreated to pass.

post pattern

n: a pass route in which the receiver runs straight downfield and then heads toward the goalpost.

power back

n: a big runner who picks up yardage because of his size and strength and not because of his speed or deception.

pressure

n: the defense's act of harassing the quarterback as he is about to pass.

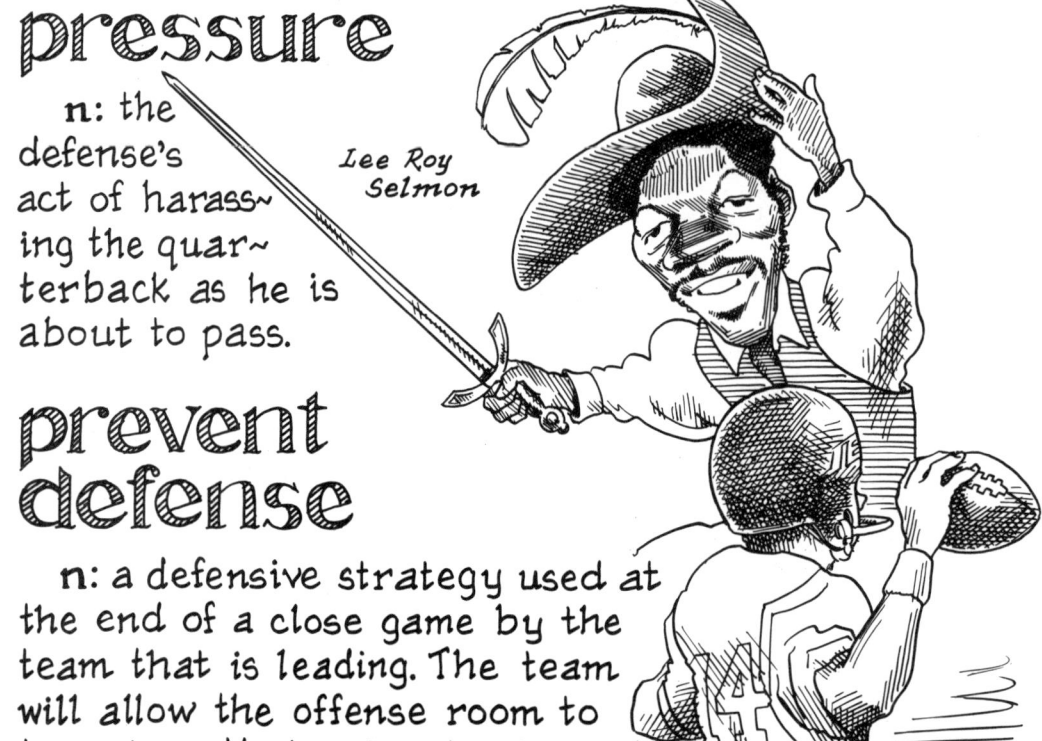

Lee Roy Selmon

prevent defense

n: a defensive strategy used at the end of a close game by the team that is leading. The team will allow the offense room to try plays that gain short~yardage but will concentrate on stopping plays that might go for a long gain. Many critics say that all this type of defense prevents is a victory for the defenders because it makes it too easy for the trailing team to get close enough for a touchdown or field goal.

pull taffy

v: to exchange the ball without getting anywhere. First one team has possession, tries three plays and kicks the ball away. Then the other team gets it and does the same thing. This continues

(pull taffy cont'd)
until the taffy breaks and one team mounts a drive and scores.

pulling guard

n: the offensive lineman who steps back as the ball is snapped and moves along the line leading the blocking for a ball carrier who is trying to find running room around the end.

punt

n: a kick made by dropping the ball and swinging your foot through it before it hits the ground. Used when a team has failed to get a first down and must give up the ball.

put the hat on

v: to hit a ballcarrier so hard that your helmet leaves an impression.

Quarterback

Dan Fouts

n: the offensive player who makes everything happen. He calls the play in the huddle; calls the signals at the line; checks the defense to see the formation; takes the snap of the ball and then either hands it off to a running back or passes it to a receiver. Nobody wins without an outstanding quarterback.

quarterback sneak

n: a running play in which the quarterback takes the snap from center, keeps the ball, and follows the center who is blocking straight ahead. This is designed for a play in which short yardage is all that's needed.

Racehorse

James Lofton

n: a receiver the defense has to worry about all the way down the field. His speed does not end a few yards beyond the line of scrimmage but continues as a fine thoroughbred's does.

read pattern

n: a pass play in which the receiver has options that he chooses once that play has begun. He checks the way the defense is moving once the play has started (the read) and then moves out to get free depending on what spaces are open (the pattern).

red chipper

n: a designation given by scouts to athletes who are good and can hurt you with their play. But you should be able to figure out a way to control them. A blue chipper can hurt you and he is usually unstoppable. A "not at all" is a player you really don't have to worry about.

red dog

n: a defensive play in which a linebacker goes

(red dog cont'd)
directly after the quarterback.

release

n: a maneuver in which a receiver (usually the tight end) navigates quickly through the traffic at the line to get free. The most important qualities a receiver can have for this are size and speed, two things no coach can teach.

Kellen Winslow

reverse

n: a play in which a ball carrier moving in one direction hands the ball off to another man moving in the opposite direction. Usually this play involves the quarterback (who takes the snap), a running back (who gets the first handoff), and a wide receiver (who is heading toward the running back and gets the ball from him, and whose outstanding speed can make this play work.)

ring the bell

v: to get hit so hard you feel as if you are vibrating

(ring the bell cont'd)
from the sound of a large bell just gonged with your head inside it.

rollout

n: a play in which the quarterback takes the snap and runs behind the line with the option of running with the ball, pitching it out to a running back trailing the play, or passing it downfield to a receiver.

rouge

n: a score worth one point in Canadian football only. A kicking team is awarded the point if one of its kicks (a punt or a kickoff) is not returned out of the end zone, which measures 25 yards as opposed to the 10-yard end zones in the United States.

roughing

part: illegally hitting a man, usually a quarterback or a kicker, after he is out of the play.

rover

n: a defensive back not assigned to a specific area who roams the field looking for the action.

run to daylight

v: to run with the ball to an open spot on the field.

running back

n: the offensive player who gets the ball on a handoff from the quarterback and tries to advance it downfield.

Sack

v: to tackle a quarterback behind the line of scrimmage.

Mark Gastineau

safety valve

n: the man the quarterback looks to (and often throws to) when he is in trouble and needs to get rid of the ball in a hurry. This player is usually near the line of scrimmage.

sandwich

v: to trap one offensive player—usually one with the ball—between two defensive players.

scramble

v: to run and dodge would-be tacklers when you, as a quarterback, have had your protective

Fran Tarkenton

(scramble cont'd)
blocking break down. Fran Tarkenton came into the league with the Minnesota Vikings in 1961 and quickly developed a reputation as a quarterback who could not be tackled. He would run as many as 25 yards back from the line of scrimmage trying to get away from tacklers so he then could head back downfield. His nickname: Fran the Scram.

screen pass

n: a short pass, usually behind the line of scrimmage, to a running back. In this play the quarterback drops back a little farther than usual, the offensive linemen let their individual opponents get through with little resistance. Then those offensive linemen move forward and form a blocking wedge for the running back who catches the pass.

scrimmage

n: any play that starts with the snap from the center; the scrimmage line is the yard line (a marked or unmarked yardline) that passes through the point of the ball nearest a team's own goal line.

secondary

n: the defensive backfield, which includes two cornerbacks and two safeties in most defensive patterns. The Green Bay secondary of Herb Adderley and Bob Jeter at cornerback, and Willie Wood and

(secondary cont'd)
Tom Brown at safety was a key reason for the Packers' victories in the first two Super Bowl games.

seam

n: an open area between two zones in a defense.

shank

v: to punt a ball off the side of the foot and have it fly erratically for only a few yards.

shed a tackler

v: to keep running and break away from a defender who has his hands on you.

George Rogers

shotgun

n: a formation in which the quarterback stands several yards behind the center and gets a direct snap. This is a passing formation used to give the quarterback more time to throw before the onrushing defense can get to him.

single wing

n: an outdated formation in which the quarterback serves as a blocking back and either the tailback or the fullback gets the direct snap from center. The single wing tailback had a role much like the quarterback of today but would be called upon to do

(single wing cont'd)

a lot more running. The wingback would be positioned outside the end but about even with the fullback and tailback. The key to success of this formation was deception, never letting any defender be quite sure where the ball was and which way it was going.

situation substitution

n: a replacement who has a specific duty at a specific time only and for specific plays. He will come out of the game as soon as that time has passed. He might be a nickel back in a passing situation, a big defensive lineman for a stand, or a fleet receiver for a long-yardage play.

skirt the end

v: to run, almost gingerly, carrying the ball around the outside of the offensive line looking for an open field and a long-gainer.

Franco Harris

slant

v: to run on an angle to and beyond the line of scrimmage.

slot

n: the position of a receiver who lines up a step behind the line and split a few yards away from the offensive tackle but inside the wide receiver on that side.

snap

n: the action of the center bringing the ball back between his legs and into the quarterback's hands.

soccer~style

Pete Gogolak

n: the method used by place~kickers who approach the ball on an angle and kick it toward the goalposts. The ball is kicked with the instep in much the same fashion as a soccer player will kick the ball to get it downfield. Kickers of this style are more accurate and get more distance than the traditional straight~ahead kickers. The first successful soccer~style kicker was Pete Gogolak who revolutionized the art of place~kicking in the mid~1960s when he first played with the Buffalo Bills. Gogolak had learned soccer from his father who escaped from Hungary in 1956. Gogolak translated his kicking skill to the football field while an undergraduate at Cornell.

spear

v: to hit and stop a runner by thrusting your helmeted head into your opponent's midsection. A dangerous and illegal maneuver.

special teams

n: the players assigned to kicking plays, either

(special teams cont'd)

when their team is receiving the ball or kicking it. At one time places on the special teams were reserved for rookies hoping to get noticed or veterans hoping to hang on. Sometimes a place would be held for the type of wild player who liked the mayhem that occurs when some twenty big athletes come hurtling down the field. But now special teams are treated with more respect and some top players play on them.

speedo

n: the ultimate compliment to a player's speed. When Bob Hayes was with the Dallas Cowboys, other players on his team and throughout the league were fast but only he was Speedo. Hayes, winner of two gold medals in the Tokyo Olympics of 1964, came to the Cowboys not having played college football. But his speed and his strength quickly made him a legend in the NFL, a legend that still lives.

spike

v: to slam the ball straight down, usually done in the end zone by a player who has just scored a touchdown.

spiral

n: the spinning motion of a thrown football that

(spiral cont'd) keeps it moving point forward and on a straight line toward a receiver.

split

n: the distance a receiver is lined up wide of his offensive tackle.

split the uprights

v: to kick a ball for a field goal or extra point so straight that it seems to be bisecting the area between the two goalposts.

squareout

n: a pass pattern in which the receiver runs about 15 yards beyond the line of scrimmage and then turns and moves in a straight line toward the sideline.

squib kick

n: a kickoff that is kicked low and short. By making the ball bounce around, it becomes harder for the receiving team to recover and return it any significant distance.

stop and go

n: a pass pattern that utilizes a receiver's speed.

(stop and go cont'd)

He takes a few steps over the line of scrimmage and then stops, hoping the defender will react and move up as if a pass is about to arrive. But the receiver, after his short stop, breaks downfield, hoping to leave the defender flatfooted.

straightarm

n: a maneuver used to fend off a tackler where the runner thrusts his arm straight out for leverage and uses his hand to push the would-be tackler out of the way.

strip the ball

Mike Haynes

v: to force a receiver to drop the ball by hitting him just as he is about to catch a pass or has just caught it.

strong safety

n: the defensive back lined up opposite the side of the offensive line containing the most players. He has the responsibility of defending against the opponent's tight end on pass plays.

strongside

n: the side of an offensive line having the most

(strongside cont'd)
players and usually including the tight end.

student-body right

Marcus Allen

n: a running play in which everybody moves in the same direction to provide interference for the ball-carrier. When Marcus Allen was at the University of Southern California, this play (or its twin brother student-body left) worked so well that he gained 2,342 yards in his senior season and won the 1981 Heisman Trophy.

stunt

n: a defensive maneuver in which players, hoping to throw the offensive linemen off stride and out of their usual blocking patterns, shift places. This also can be effective because defenders charge in toward the ballcarrier at unusual angles.

stutter step

n: a quick move made by changing the timing, length, and direction of your stride in an effort to get a defender to stop or move in the wrong direction.

submarine

v: to tackle a ball-carrier by hitting him low,

(submarine cont'd)
usually around the ankles. If this works the runner spins in the air as he heads for the turf. If it doesn't work the tackler is left with a mouthful of field and the ball carrier can run for a gain.

sudden death

n: the overtime period in a professional football game. If a playoff game is tied at the end of four quarters, the teams keep playing regulation 15-minute quarters until one scores; as soon as one team scores it wins and the other team is dead. In regular-season play, a tie at the end of four quarters goes to a sudden-death period, but there is only one extra quarter. A tie at the end of a fifth quarter, is a tie in the record books. The most famous sudden-death game was the 1958 National Football League championship between the Baltimore Colts and the New York Giants. This was the first time a pro football championship had gone into overtime. It was a nationally televised game that included some of the sport's brightest stars. When the Colts rallied to tie on Steve Myra's field goal and win in overtime on Alan Ameche's short run, millions of fans were converted to the religion of pro football on Sundays.

suicide squad

n: another name for kicking teams and one which accurately captures the nature of play on

(suicide squad cont'd)
kicking situations with powerful, finely conditioned athletes flinging themselves fearlessly at one another.

Super Bowl

n: the biggest game of the pro football year, the National Football League championship. The Super Bowl was first played in 1967 and followed the 1966 peace treaty that led to the merger of the National Football League and the American Football League. After competing for players and fans for six years the two leagues hammered out an agreement that called for a common draft of players, an understanding that teams would honor player contracts, a complete merger of the two leagues by 1970, and a championship game to be played each January. The first game was clumsily called the AFL-NFL World Championship Game. That contest was won by Vince Lombardi's Green Bay Packers as was the second championship. By the time Joe Namath's Jets played in the third championship game, the name Super Bowl had been popularized. But the ease with which the Packers had won the first two titles threatened to make the final game an anticlimax as it seemed the older NFL teams were far superior to the AFL teams. But Namath & Co. changed that and firmly implanted the Super Bowl in America's consciousness.

Joe Namath

sweep

n: a running play in which the offensive line moves out towards the sideline and the ball carrier follows behind them.

swim

v: to use your arms almost as if you were doing the Australian crawl. Employed by tight ends or defensive linemen in an effort to get by a man trying to stop them.

Ozzie Newsome

swing pass

n: a short pass thrown quickly to a back on either side of the quarterback.

swivel hips

n: what a player who is particularly hard to get hold of and tackle seems to have.

Ottis Anderson

Tackle

v: to stop a ball-carrier and force him to the ground.
n: the offensive line position, outside the guards but inside the ends, that is usually most responsible for protecting the quarterback; the defensive line positions that are in the center of a four-man line.

tailback

n: the running back set up farther from the line of scrimmage than any other. In the "I" formation he is the deep back.

tank

n: a big running back who is about as easy to tackle as one of those vehicles that rumbled across Europe following D-Day.

Tank Younger

taxi squad

n: a group of players who don't quite make a pro football team but aren't quite bad enough to be sent packing completely. These players practice with the team and often are paid by the team, but they are not permitted by league rules to suit up for games. The term derives from the onetime owner of the Cleveland Browns, Mickey McBride, the owner of a fleet of cabs. In the 40s, players who were not quite good enough to make the Browns were given a job driving one of McBride's cabs to keep them available in case injuries or other problems arose.

T formation

n: an offensive set in which the quarterback is directly behind the center and the running backs are in a straight line behind the quarterback and parallel to the offensive line. If there are three running backs the set is called a fullhouse

(T formation cont'd)

backfield; if there are only two running backs with the other back split out as a wide receiver, it's called a split T. The T formation became popular when Clark Shaughnessy taught it to the Chicago Bears in 1940. It can be effective equally on running plays or passing plays.

throw into a crowd

v: to pass into a group of potential receivers and potential interceptors where the chance is slim that any offensive player will be able to catch the ball.

throw it away

v: to pass the ball safely out of the reach of any defender when all of your potential receivers are covered. The exact opposite of throwing into a crowd.

tight end

n: the receiver position occupied by a big, fast, and durable player. He must be able to block for running plays since he is usually set up right next to an offensive tackle; he must be fast enough and shifty enough to get free when running a pass route; and he must be durable enough to stand up to the beating he takes while blocking.

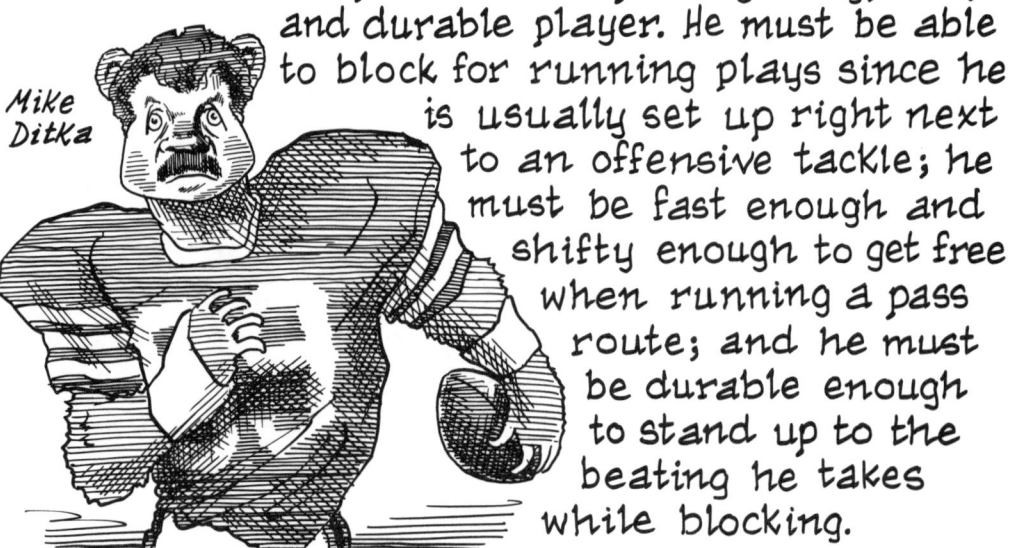

Mike Ditka

tightrope

n: the sideline. To walk the tightrope is to run along the sideline without letting your feet touch the stripe. If you do, you're out of bounds and the play is stopped.

touch football

n: the schoolyard, backyard, or park game made famous by the Kennedy family. In this game, no tackling is permitted. The ball carrier is stopped when he is touched by both hands of a defensive player. Since it is fairly simple to stop a player who is running with the ball by touching him, the offense in these games is usually the result of passing. A touch football game can be played with anywhere from 2 to 11 on a side.

Alfred Jenkins

touchback

n: a ball that is downed in the end zone by the receiving team following a kickoff, punt, interception, or fumble recovery. The team that downed the ball gets possession of it at its 20-yard line.

touchdown

n: six points awarded for carrying the ball across the goal line or receiving a pass in the end zone.

trap

v: to allow a defensive lineman to penetrate the

Sammy Baugh

(trap cont'd) offensive line only to be blocked once he has gotten through. The ball carrier then runs through the area the defender has been blocked away from.

triple-threat back

n: a player who could run, pass, or kick. In these days of specialization, there are few backs around with all of these skills at a high level. A great triple-threat back was Sammy Baugh, who was the quarterback of the Washington Redskins from 1937 to 1952. He was so good at running, passing, and punting that he was one of seventeen charter members when the Pro Football Hall of Fame was created in 1963.

Turk

n: the man who tells pro football players that they are about to be cut. The bearer of the bad news is a "Turk" because the word conjures an image of a man wielding a small curved sword known as a scimitar and used to cut a swath. The Turk is usually an equipment manager, a low-ranking assistant coach or the son of the team general manager. Most head coaches break the news to the player but they like to have someone else get them ready—The Turk. He comes to a player after practice and says, "Coach wants to see you and bring your playbook." That can

(Turk cont'd)
only mean one thing. Telling a player he isn't good enough can get a little chancy. In the preseason of 1983, Frank Kush, head coach of the Baltimore Colts, told Holden Smith, a wide receiver, that he had been loafing through a practice drill and was being released. Smith retaliated by dumping a container of root beer on the coach's head. Four days before the 1984 USFL season began, John Hadl, the coach of the Los Angeles Express told Greg Fields, a big defensive end, that he wasn't going to make the team. Before some assistant coaches outside the office could pull Fields away from Hadl, the coach had a black eye and a welt on his forehead.

turn in

n: a pass pattern in which the receiver runs a few yards downfield and then cuts straight across toward the middle of the field

turn it over

v: to get a punt to go slowly end over end in the air, giving the kick more distance and making it more difficult for the punt returner to catch it.

two-minute drill

n: a series of plays set up during practice for the last two minutes of the first half or the last

Roger Staubach

(two-minute drill cont'd) two minutes of the game. A team will know which of its plays will be called depending on the situation. This keeps a team from having to waste precious seconds in the huddle or precious timeouts figuring out the fastest way to go the farthest in the least amount of time.

two-minute warning

n: a timeout called by the officials in a professional game with two minutes left in the first or second half. It lets a coach know (in case he was ignoring the scoreboard clock) that his two-minute offense is about to go to work. It also gives the networks televising the game a chance to get a few more commercials on the air.

two-way player

n: a player who is adept both on offense and defense and spends time playing on both. The last great two-way player was Chuck Bednarik, who went from a career as a center and linebacker for the Philadelphia Eagles into the pro football hall of fame. In recent seasons, Roy Green of the St. Louis Cardinals caused a stir by making the team as defensive back but spending time as a

Chuck Bednarik

(two-way player cont'd)
wide receiver. He was so talented a pass-catcher that he was switched and is now one of the best in the NFL.

Underneath
n: the area in front of the greatest concentration of defensive backs and linebackers.

uprights
n: the vertical bars rising from the crossbar on the goal posts. In the NFL, these bars rise thirty feet in the air to help the officials determine whether a kick has gone between them and therefore is good.

Veer

n: an offensive style used mostly in colleges, devised by Bill Yeomans of Houston. It takes advantage of some elusive running backs and protects against offensive linemen who aren't the world's best blockers. This is basically a triple option offense usually run from an "I" formation. After the snap, the quarterback decides what to do, according to the way the defense reacts. He can give to the fullback plunging straight ahead; he can move along the line and pitch to his tailback, or he can keep the ball. Actually, it is a quadruple option

(veer cont'd)
because when the quarterback decides to keep, he can run or pass.

vertical passing game

n: an offense that features a lot of long passes straight downfield aimed at producing big gains. This is the type of offense favored by the Los Angeles Raiders over the years. The keys are a strong-armed quarterback (Daryle Lamonica, Ken Stabler, and Jim Plunkett) and fleet receivers (Warren Wells and Cliff Branch).

Ken Stabler

Weakside

n: the side of the offense or defense with fewer players. On the offense, this is the side away from the tight end. On defense it's the side away from the strong safety.

wedge

n: a group of blockers, usually on a kickoff return who form a V shape in front of the kick returner.

wide receiver

n: the player farthest out along or just behind the line of scrimmage. The position was formerly

(wide receiver cont'd)

Known as flankerback or split end. These players are fast and sure-handed and responsible for catching passes of at least 15 yards or more.

wild card

n: a team that makes the pro playoffs without finishing first in its division. There are four wild cards awarded each season in the NFL. They go to the two teams with the best records in each conference that did not win their division titles. Because of the parity of so many NFL teams, the fact that a club has no chance to win the division with a few weeks left in the season doesn't mean it cannot qualify for the playoffs and a shot at the Super Bowl. It heightens fan interest and sometimes rewards a deserving team. In 1980, the Oakland Raiders qualified for the playoffs as a wild card and swept to victory in Super Bowl XV.

wingback

n: a position manned by a running back who is split away from the other running backs but not so far that he cannot come towards the quarterback for a handoff and not so close that he can't get up to the line for a flare or screen pass. He is also responsible for blocking when the tailback runs.

Ron Springs

wishbone

n: a formation used by many colleges to take advantage of the running skills of the quarterback. In this formation the quarterback lines up directly behind the center with three backs behind him. One is about five yards directly behind the quarterback. The other two are a few yards farther back and split apart from each other. Seen from above, the backfield forms the letter Y and it also resembles the shape of a chicken's wishbone. The quarterback, after taking the snap from center, will run either right or left with two of the backs leading him for additional blocking and with the third back trailing the play. If the quarterback sees he has a clear path he takes off upfield. If he does not have a clear path, he tosses the ball back to one of the trailing backs. The system was devised by Emory Bellard when he was an assistant coach at Texas A&M and it was perfected when he became an assistant to Darrell Royal at the University of Texas.

Zone

n: a pass defense in which each player is responsible for one area on the field and not specifically assigned to cover a man

NICKNAMES

Some football players had nicknames that sounded like the names of old railroad trains—Old No. 98. Or stemmed from some youthful incident—Hacksaw. Or a mistake—Wrong Way. But one thing about football players, the nickname usually makes the man and says it all about him. If I say, "The Bear," you say, "Bryant." And so on.

Lance (**Bambi**) Alworth

As a rookie with the San Diego Chargers, a teammate, Charlie Flowers, took one look at Alworth and named him Bambi after the deer in the Walt Disney animated movie. Flowers gave him the name "because of your big brown eyes and the way you run." But this was no frightened fawn at wide receiver. After he retired he had set records for catching touchdown passes in 96 straight games and became the first American Football League player elected to the Pro Football Hall of Fame.

Lance Alworth

Slingin' Sammy Baugh

He practiced passing with the aid of an automobile tire hanging from ropes tied to the branch of a tree. His brother pushed the tire so it swung back and forth pendulum-style. Baugh threw passes through the swinging tire, getting so good at it that he could do it on the run. But his nickname is traced to the strong arm he displayed while playing third base in high school. Amos Melton, a writer for the Fort Worth *Star Telegram* watched him fire the ball from

(Sammy Baugh cont'd)
third to first and quickly named him Slingin' Sam.

Paul (**Bear**) Bryant

It was near his boyhood home in Moro Bottom, Arkansas that the coach with the most college victories got his name. He was then a 6-foot-4-inch teenager who "wasn't very smart in school, and lazy to boot." This is how he recalled that day: "It was outside the Lyric Theater. There was a poster out front with a picture of a bear and someone was offering a dollar a minute to anyone who would wrestle the bear. The guy who was supposed to do it didn't show up so they egged me on. I wrestled this scrawny bear to the floor. I went around later to get my money, but the guy with the bear had flown the coop. All I got out of the whole thing was a nickname.

Dave (**The Ghost**) Casper

Named by his Oakland Raider teammates as a take-off on the cartoon character, Casper the Friendly Ghost. But the shade of his skin also contributed to it. "Casper is the whitest white person I have ever seen," said Jack Tatum.

Mean Joe Greene

Charles Edward Greene attended North Texas State University and was the leader of a tough defensive unit named "The Mean Green" for its green jerseys. He was the toughest player on that unit and got the name "Mean Joe" as a result. He never liked it for he felt it branded him as a dirty player. He was not but through his career with the Pittsburgh Steelers he was always the toughest player on the Steelers' tough defense.

Tom (Old No. 98) Harmon

When he reported for his first practice at Horace Mann High in Gary, Indiana, Harmon was told to "pick a uniform and get out on the field." He took a uniform that was meant for a regular, not a scrawny 14-year-old freshman. The coach sent him back. He found the shabbiest jersey and wore it. When Harmon's skill became apparent, the coach told him to change his number, but the youngster never would. He remained No. 98 throughout his career. During World War II Harmon was a fighter pilot who survived two plane crashes — once over Surinam and once over China. Each time Harmon emerged, the first time after being missing for 10 days, the second time after a month. And 98 must have been his lucky number, for both planes bore the logo, *Little Butch 98*.

Elroy (Crazylegs) Hirsch

Elroy Hirsch

Growing up in Wausau, Wisconsin, Elroy Hirsch ran home two miles from school each day, skipping and crisscrossing his legs. He said it would make him shiftier. He developed the same style of running in games and the Wausau High fans were enthralled and began calling him Crazylegs.

Paul (Golden Boy) Hornung

His wavy blond hair, green eyes and boyish good looks won this name while a quarterback at Notre Dame. After joining the Green Bay Packers, Hornung couldn't get along with his coach, Lisle Blackbourn. The team was losing so Blackbourn sarcastically renamed Hornung the Golden Dome.

David (Deacon) Jones

While attending college at South Carolina State, David Jones led the football squad in prayer before each game. For his efforts he was named "Deacon." "I like that name," he has said. "People remember it when they wouldn't remember David." Through a 14-year pro career with the Los Angeles Rams and the San Diego Chargers as a defensive lineman, no one forgot it.

Ed (Too Tall) Jones

After playing some varsity basketball at Tennessee State, the 6-foot-9-inch Jones began playing football. A teammate took one look at the big newcomer and said, "Man, you're too tall to play football." His defensive line play for the Dallas Cowboys proves that he wasn't.

Dick (Night Train) Lane

Every day after practice with the Los Angeles Rams, the young Dick Lane would visit the room of the Rams' great pass receiver, Tom Fears. Fears liked to play music in his room, and his favorite was the instrumental, "Night Train." "Everytime I would go to his room he would be playing it. He roomed with a player named Ben Sheets." When Lane visited the room Sheets said, "here comes that Night Train again."

Gene (Big Daddy) Lipscomb

The first defensive lineman to gain notoriety for his flamboyant lifestyle and outstanding play. He was a star with the Baltimore Colts when they won two NFL titles in the late 1950s. He started his pro career with

(Gene Lipscomb cont'd)
the Los Angeles Rams and it was there that he got his nickname. He began calling each teammate "Little Daddy." In turn, they called the 6-foot-6-inch, 290-pound Lipscomb "Big Daddy."

Carl (Spider) Lockhart

While playing free safety with the New York Giants, Lockhart's defensive backfield coach was Emlen Tunnell, a hall of fame defensive back. In Lockhart's rookie season of 1965 Tunnell took a look at his star pupil and said, "he was all over those guys like a spider."

Hugh (The King) McElhenny

It was 1952 and Hugh McElhenny had just joined the San Francisco 49ers from the University of Washington. ("The only college player in history who took a salary cut to turn pro," said the team's quarterback Frankie Albert.) One of McElhenny's first games was against the Chicago Bears and he fielded a punt on the 6-yard line, twisted and squirmed and ran through the Bears for 94 yards and a touchdown. He finished the game with 283 yards of total offense and afterwards George Halas, the Bear coach said, "That was the damndest greatest run I've ever seen in football." He's the King," Albert said. "McElhenny's the King of runners."

John (Blood) McNally

In 1924 McNally and a friend heard that a professional team was looking for players. Both men had college eligibility left so they decided to use pseudonyms. While walking to tryouts they saw a theater marquee advertising the latest Rudolph Valentino hit, "Blood and Sand." McNally turned to his friend and said, "That's it. You be Sand and I'll be Blood."

Walter (Sweetness) Payton

His teammates in the 1975 Senior Bowl gave him the name, both for his sweet running style and his sweet disposition.

Jack (Hacksaw) Reynolds

His University of Tennessee team was beaten by Mississippi, 38-0, in a game that kept Tennessee from a Sugar Bowl berth. In frustration, Reynolds bought a hacksaw and 13 blades and cut his 1953 Chevrolet in half. After eight hours he had two pieces of a Chevrolet and 13 broken blades. When he took friends to see his deed, he found only the 13 broken blades. He never found out what happened to the car.

Walter Payton

Roy (Wrong Way) Riegels

In the 1929 Rose Bowl, Riegels, the 170-pound center of the University of California picked up a Georgia Tech fumble and ran toward the goal line — the *wrong* goal line. By the time he realized what he had done, California was deep in its own territory and Georgia Tech was on its way to a safety and an 8-7 victory.

Gale (Magic) Sayers

His incredible knack of getting into the end zone led Ed McCaskey, an executive of the Chicago Bears and George Halas's son-in-law, to name Sayers "Black Magic," later shortened to just "Magic."

Kenny (Snake) Stabler

As a high school freshman in Foley, Alabama, he ran back a punt 70 yards for a touchdown. But he zigged and zagged and twisted so much, he covered twice that amount of yardage. His excited coach said, "Boy you ran just like a snake."

Jack (The Assassin) Tatum

When the Oakland Raiders signed Tatum as a defensive back out of Ohio State they issued a press release that said, "The Oakland Raiders have just hired the Assassin no winning team could be without." "I didn't like the name," Tatum said in his book, *They Call Me Assassin*. "I thought that makes me sound like a gangster. But actually I was a hit man." He became a controversial figure when one of his hits broke the neck of Darryl Stingley, leaving the New England Patriots' player paralyzed for life. Tatum's friends call him the Reverend.

Byron (Whizzer) White

His brother, Sam, had preceded him at the University of Colorado and when White got there he was known as "Sam White's Brother." But Byron quickly showed that he was a better football player than Sam had been. A sportswriter for *The Rocky Mountain News*, Leonard Kahn, felt that this marvelous player needed a more appealing name than Byron and conjured the alliterative Whizzer White. Following his graduation from Colorado in 1938 he had a choice between a Rhodes Scholarship and a chance to play professionally with the Pittsburgh Steelers. He took Pittsburgh not Oxford, at least for a while. "How can I refuse an offer like that?" he said. "It will pay my way through law school." But he did take his Rhodes scholarship too and while in England he met a 21-year-old Harvard student named John Kennedy, the son of the American Ambassador. Their friendship continued over the years. White retired from football in 1941 (having attended

(Byron White cont'd)
law school throughout his playing days). Twenty years later President John F. Kennedy appointed Whizzer White to the United States Supreme Court.

Justice "Whizzer" White

WALTER CAMP

The captain of the Harvard football team (1876) looked across at the Yale team, sized up their players and walked over to the Yale captain.

"You don't mean to let that child play do you?" the Harvard man asked. "He is too light. He will get hurt."

"Look to your business," said the Yalie. "He is young, but he is all spirit and whipcord."

Walter Camp, 6-feet 157 pounds of spirit and whipcord, heard the interchange. He remained cool. But early in the game, when the Harvard captain, Nathaniel Curtis, was running with the ball, Camp, staying within the rules of the day, grabbed Curtis and threw him to the ground. Curtis got up slowly and looked at the Yale captain, Gene Baker.

"You're right," Curtis said. "That little fellow nearly put me out."

And so the man who was called the "Father of American Football" began his 50-year association with Yale and football.

This was only the second meeting between Yale and Harvard. The previous year Harvard easily had won the first game and was heavily favored to win the second.

But the Yale men understood this new game much better than they had the year before. "We were on the side of men who want no chance of retreat or escape, only a fair contest and certain victory or defeat at the end of it," Camp recalled. "To what do all the technicalities amount when compared with the sincerity of men who come together to effect that result?"

Yale won the game, one goal to none.

Camp's paternal title was well-deserved. He devised the down system and the scrimmage line with one team having possession. Previously the ball was just thrown down between the two teams and they clawed and fought for it until one gained the advantage and advanced the ball. This resembled rugby and was a far more dangerous game. Camp turned the sport into one today's fans might recognize.

But before he did his inventing he played the game. He was a halfback at Yale for six full seasons and part of a seventh. There was no pro football then and since Camp remained a student at Yale's medical school, he stayed on the team. An injury in 1882 ended his career. During Camp's playing days, Yale won twenty five, lost only one, and tied six. For three of those seasons he was the team captain.

Yale's only loss was to Princeton in 1878, a loss Camp attributed to bad living. "The Blue," Camp said, "went back to New Haven with a very salutary lesson on the evil of neglecting the laws of training."

As a creator of football rules, Walter Camp believed in the principle of evolution and never advocated startling innovation, founding each new development on what had gone before.

"If Walter Camp had contributed not a single thing else to football," Tom Cohane wrote in his *The Yale Football Story,* "his name would still rest secure on the scrimmage, perhaps the greatest single invention in any game. From the scrimmage evolved the set play, the sequence of plays, the strategy."

At a rules committee meeting in 1882, Camp offered his second great contribution that basically said, "If in three downs a team shall not have advanced the ball five yards or lost ten, they must give up the ball to the other side." That has evolved into four downs to advance the ball ten yards but the basic structure of the game had been just about set.

"How do you propose to tell when five yards have been made?" Camp was asked.

"We shall have to rule off the field," said Camp, "with horizontal chalked lines every five yards."

"The field will look like a gridiron," someone else said.

"Precisely," Camp responded.

It did not end there. Camp gave up his study of medicine ("I can't bear the sight of blood") and went to work for a watch company. That was his work. His life was football. He is generally given credit with choosing the first all-America team in 1889, a practice he continued until his death.

On that first all-America team was a Yale guard named William (Pudge) Heffelfinger. Heffelfinger was on the next three of Camp's all-star teams and to this day is always mentioned when anyone puts together an all-time all-America squad. Among Camp's other disciples was Amos Alonzo

Stagg, who coached college football for 56 years and was still involved in the game at his death at the age of 102.

Camp's prize was Heffelfinger and though he wasn't nearly the size of the modern offensive lineman (he weighed 205 pounds) his tactics very much resembled the guards of today. "Heffelfinger was the fastest big man I ever saw," Camp said. "He not only could cover his own position but a good part of space of the tackle or center and he was the most effective man in leading interference out around end that I ever saw come out of a line position or any position." The first pulling guard.

So Walter Camp devised the down and the scrimmage; he picked the first all-Americans; he served as the first true coach; he nurtured the great Pudge Heffelfinger and Alonzo Stagg. But that was not all. One day in 1892 Camp received a letter that would have a profound effect on the future of college football.

Dear Sir:

I want to ask a favor of you. Will you kindly furnish me with some points on the best way to develop a good football team. I am an instructor connected with this university and have been asked to coach the team. I know something of the rugby game, but would like to find out the best manner to handle the men. I have seen a good many Yale games (as I come from New Haven, you can find out about me from Dr. Seaver) and knowing you are an authority on the game, I would welcome any points you might give me. Hoping that I am not asking too great a favor of you,

Your sincere admirer,
James H. Kivlan
University of Notre Dame
Notre Dame, Indiana

Camp, naturally, helped and Notre Dame put the advice to good use.

Walter Camp never stopped reinventing football. To keep the offenses in check, he devised new tactics for the defenses. When the defenses were becoming too dominant he devised new offensive tactics. When the college game became far too dangerous and President Theodore Roosevelt threatened to outlaw football in 1906, Camp served on the committee that devised the rules to save the game and its players.

Walter Camp died in New York in March of 1925 while attending a rules committee meeting.

KNUTE ROCKNE

When Knute Rockne was killed in an airplane crash in a Kansas wheatfield, the nation mourned. It was March 31, 1931, and the United States was stumbling through the first years of the Great Depression. One continuum of success, however, was the Notre Dame football team and the Irish's great coach, Rockne. But when Rockne's plane went down, it gave the whole country a jolt.

"We are becoming so hardened by misfortune and bad luck that it takes a mighty big calamity to shock all this country," the humorist Will Rogers said. "But Knute, you did it. We thought it would take a president's death to make a whole nation shake its head in real sorrow and say, 'Ain't it a shame he's gone?' Well, that's what this country did today, Knute, for you. You died one of our national heroes. Notre Dame was your address but every gridiron in America was your home."

Indeed it was. Knute Rockne was born in Voss, Norway in 1888. His father, a carriagemaker, came to Chicago in 1893, found success and sent for his family. Knute quickly learned about American sports. His father was no longer so successful and when it came time for college, Knute couldn't afford to go. He stayed home for a few years and then one day some friends told him of their plan to attend Notre Dame.

"Notre Dame?" Rockne said. "What's Notre Dame?"

He found out. In 1910 he went to the school in South Bend, Indiana and never left. He was a chemistry major and quite a good student. But he gained fame as an end who, with the quarterback Gus Dorais, combined on the forward pass so proficiently as to upset a favored Army team. Passing had been legalized seven years before, but it was that day in 1913 at West Point that many football historians point to as the beginning of the modern passing game. Rockne and Dorais had spent the previous summer as lifeguards and that was when the genius of Rockne as a football mind first became evident.

"We've been taught to catch a ball against our chest," Rockne told Dorais. "That's unnatural. There's no give to a man's chest. The ball has a tendency to bounce off. A baseball outfielder softens the impact of the catch by giving with his hands. Maybe a football should be caught the same way."

It worked. Notre Dame stunned Army, 35-13.

Rockne stayed at Notre Dame after graduation as an assistant to Coach Jess Harper. Then in 1918 he became head coach. He made his presence known immediately to the Notre Dame publicity man.

"I'm running this team. Nobody else has anything to say about its makeup or play. If it's a flop, pan me."

That time never came. In 13 seasons his teams won 105 games, lost 12, and tied 5. He had five unbeaten seasons. And as much as anybody could Knute Rockne won because of his words.

He was born a Lutheran but converted to Catholicism in 1925. For years, he said, he was "a lone Norse Protestant in a stronghold of Irish Catholics." The day he converted was also the day of a Notre Dame-Northwestern game. At halftime, the Irish trailed, 10-0, and Rockne told his players, "This is a hell of a religion you got me into. On my first day in it you let yourself be pushed around by a Methodist school."

Notre Dame won, 13-10.

Another time his team was losing at halftime, Rockne poked his head into the locker room and all he said was, "Fighting Irish. Bah!" They won that one, too.

His most famous team was the 1924 squad led by the backfield forever immortalized by the writer Grantland Rice as The Four Horsemen—Don Miller, Elmer Layden, Jim Crowley, and Harry Stuhldreher. The team lost only one game in the three years the Four Horsemen were together.

But he never let the backs get carried away with their success. He always had praise for his linemen, known as the Seven Mules. "Without the Mules," he told them, "you Horsemen are just turtles."

His most famous player was George Gipp, a running back who was on the varsity team when Rockne arrived. Gipp's lifestyle did not exactly fit the Rockne way, but for a player of that quality even Rockne made an exception. In his senior year, Gipp took ill with a throat infection and died. In what has become the most famous football speech ever given, Gipp

supposedly called for Rockne as he lay near death. "Some day," Gipp said, "when things are wrong and the breaks are beating the boys, tell them to go in there with all they've got and win one for the Gipper."

Eight years later, the Irish were stumbling through their worst season under Rockne. They were playing Army at Yankee Stadium in New York and were tied, 0-0. Rockne came in and asked that team to "win this one for the Gipper." They did.

"Rockne was capable of having invented the Gipp request," it was written years later. "But Gipp was also capable of having made the request."

He spent his offseasons planning football plays and giving inspirational talks. He was hired by the Studebaker Corporation for six speeches for their sales staff.

The Rock had a list of 25 commandments that identifed "the correct mental qualifications of an athlete." Here are some of them:

> On scholarship: "The player should first be a good student. Do not neglect your studies. Your first purpose should be to get an education."
>
> On co-operation: "Everyone should work for the common good of the school and the squad. Everyone should boost everyone else; a disorganizer has no place on the squad."
>
> On attendance: "Anything worth doing is worth doing well. Try not to miss a day of school or practice."
>
> On losing: "You can be a hard but good loser. Any coach or team that cannot lose and treat their opponents with respect has no right to win; a poor sportsman generally tries to amuse the spectators with his self-styled clever wit by making abusive remarks, which act as a boomerang by intelligent spectators."
>
> On winning: "If you are the rightful winner, be willing to take credit for it, but keep in mind that it was only your time to win and that your winning was probably due to conditions or a reward for your sacrifices; a kind word or a handshake goes a long way toward forming a lasting friendship, and does not change the score."

GEORGE HALAS

If every creation needs just one creator, then pro football's was George Stanley Halas. Over the years Halas became known as Papa Bear for his role as founder, player, coach, and owner of the Chicago Bears. It was at a meeting organized by Halas in a Canton, Ohio, automobile showroom in 1920 that the National Football League got its start.

"In 1920 paid football was pretty much of a catch-as-catch-can affair," Halas wrote in his autobiography, *Halas by Halas*. "Teams appeared one week and disappeared the next. Players came and went, drawn by the pleasure of playing. If others came to watch, that was fine. If they bought tickets or tossed coins into a helmet passed by the most popular player, that was helpful. "I thought my team, the Decatur Staleys, had gone beyond this mobile situation. We needed an organization."

The Staleys were named for A.E. Staley, a manufacturer of starch in Decatur, Illinois. Halas was the athletic director and an engineer for the starch company and he was having trouble putting together a schedule. He wrote a letter to Ralph Hay, manager of the Canton (Ohio) Bulldogs suggesting that several of these industrial teams get together and form a league. The formative meeting was in Hay's Hupmobile showroom in Canton. "Chairs were few," Halas recalled. "I sat on a running board."

Twelve teams were given franchises in the league called the American Professional Football Association, the legendary Jim Thorpe was named as president, a fee of $100 was charged (although Halas has said no money changed hands), and America had the beginnings pro football.

In 1921 the Bears moved from Decatur to Chicago. The league's name was changed to the National Football League in 1923. Until his death in 1983, George Halas was a centerpiece on the pro football scene.

The son of a Czechoslovak tailor who grew up in Chicago, Halas attended the University of Illinois where his coach was Bob Zuppke. It might have been Zuppke who sowed the seed of pro football in Halas's mind.

"Why is it," Zuppke said at a team dinner during Halas's senior season of 1917, "that just as my players begin to learn something about football, I lose them to graduation?" When Halas enlisted in the navy he had reason to think more about what Zuppke said. Halas was assigned to the Great Lakes Naval Training Station where he played end on a team that was so good, it played in the Rose Bowl.

"Zup was right," said Halas. "Post-graduate football is better football."

Zuppke's words and Halas's idea have evolved into a billion-dollar industry.

And through it all there was George Halas. He was a baseball player who signed with the Yankees. Sliding on one of his two major league hits, he injured a hip and was replaced in right field by a young slugger named Babe Ruth. But football was his true love. He savored it as few others did. When Walter Payton rushed for 275 yards in a game on a Sunday in 1977, setting a National Football League record, Halas was disappointed, for the Bears were playing again on Thursday, Thanksgiving Day.

"Something like what Walter did Sunday you usually enjoy for a whole week. But not this time damn it. I wish we weren't playing the Lions so soon, so we could savor what Walter did a little longer."

Halas loved it all. He loved a play he made in an early game between the Bears and the Canton Bulldogs.

"I'd say I made the longest touchdown run in history. It must have been 200 yards. Jim Thorpe was with Canton and he kept slashing away in an effort to break a scoreless tie. He worked the ball down to our 2 yard line. But just as he plunged over for the touchdown, I punched the ball out of his arms, scooped it up, and headed downfield. Thorpe was the maddest Indian you ever saw. He set after me and he could run like a deer. I zig-zagged from one sideline to the other. Since I couldn't outrun him, I had to outfox him.

"At the 10-yard-line, he let go and hit me with a fierce tackle. He hit me so hard that I skidded into the end zone with Thorpe riding me for the only touchdown in the game. I thought he would strangle me."

He loved Red Grange, who became pro football's first big star when Halas signed him in November 1925 following completion of Grange's college career at Illinois. Four days after he signed, Grange and the Bears played the Chicago Cardinals. The game was the Bears' first sellout in

Wrigley Field. A tour the Bears took with Grange that fall and winter drew huge crowds everywhere.

"I knew that Grange was the box-office shot in the arm pro football needed. It was the tremendous publicity generated by the Grange tour that established pro football as a national sport."

He loved his teams known as the Monsters of the Midway, the ones that moved so skillfully in the T formation that Halas helped perfect. The high point for those Bear teams came on December 8, 1940, in the NFL championship game against the Washington Redskins. Earlier that season the Redskins had beaten the Bears, 7-3, and Halas's team complained that a poor call by an official had cost it a touchdown. The Redskins called the Bears "a bunch of crybabies" and the Redskin owner, George Preston Marshall, said Chicago was strictly a first-half team.

"I had no difficulty preparing the Bears mentally for the rematch," Halas recalled. "The crybaby taunt took care of that." The Bears scored on their second play from scrimmage. At the half the score was 28-0.

"During the intermission I reminded our players that George Marshall had characterized the Bears as a first-half ball club." Seven touchdowns later the "first-half crybabies" were champions by a score of 73-0. When people said the Bears had unnecessarily poured it on, Halas responded, "We used 33 men and the 33d scored a touchdown. Should I have rushed out and tackled him myself?"

He was unfailing in helping his players after they left the team even though he was such a tough negotiator that one of his players, the great tight end Mike Ditka said, "Halas throws nickels around like manhole covers." In 1981, Halas threw enough manhole covers Ditka's way to sign him as coach.

Halas coached the Bears himself for four separate 10-year tenures. He won eight NFL titles. He owned the team for 63 years and he didn't stop coaching until arthritis in the hip he had injured playing baseball caused him to quit in 1968. "I knew it was time to stop when I started to go after an official walking along the sideline and I couldn't keep up with him."

But his love affair with the game never stopped. He was 68 when his Bear team won its last league title. "There isn't room for many of these things in one lifetime," he said. But when asked if he was going to quit, he responded, "Where's a 68-year-old man going to find a job anyway?"

RED GRANGE

October 19, 1924, is one of the most important dates in football history. It was on that day in Champaign, Illinois, that Harold (Red) Grange of the University of Illinois scored five touchdowns—four of them on long runs in the first 12 minutes—in a game against the University of Michigan. Not only did Grange stand the college football world on its ear with that performance, but he made a promoter named C.C. Pyle take notice. The game was to be forever changed.

For Pyle saw in Red Grange the kind of player the infant sport of professional football needed for it to take off. The next year he approached Grange, who was viewing a movie at one of Pyle's theaters near the Illinois campus.

"Red, how would you like to make a hundred thousand dollars, maybe even a million?" C.C. Pyle asked.

"Well yes," said Grange. "On the up and up?"

"Playing football," said Pyle. "I believe I can work out a deal with the Bears for you to go on tour with them after your last game here. It will be the biggest thing the country has ever seen."

The next week Grange was told, "Charley Pyle has just made you a very wealthy man." Pyle had struck a deal with George Halas of the Chicago Bears in which Grange would join the Bears for a barnstorming tour and Grange would share in the profits. When the country reacted as Pyle had predicted, pro football was on its way.

"I had the feeling people would have been happier if I had joined the Capone Gang," Grange recalled years later. "Bob Zuppke, my coach at Illinois, didn't speak to me for four years."

But the fans turned out. The watershed game took place in the Polo Grounds in New York on December 6, 1925. The crowd was announced at 65,000 and Grange's (and Halas's) Bears defeated the New York Giants, 14-7, with Grange scoring one touchdown and intercepting a pass.

"Up to then," Grange said, "pro ball might get three paragraphs among the truss ads. In New York four writers—Grantland Rice, Westbrook Pegler, Damon Runyon, and Ford Frick—joined us on the tour."

Pro football came into its own on the slim shoulders of this man, first called the Galloping Ghost by Warren Brown of *The Chicago Tribune.* His performance against Michigan, coming on the dedication day of Illinois Stadium, is still recalled as one of the best individual performances in sports history. Grange ran back the opening kickoff 95 yards. In the next 12 minutes he scored on runs of 67, 56, and 44 yards. He scored again later in the game.

"I was a student at Notre Dame when he was at Illinois," the columnist Red Smith once said. "I hated Grange. We had the Four Horsemen and Red was better than all of them."

A Michigan fan and reporter who tried to play down Grange's five-touchdown performance, wrote, "All Red Grange can do is run." To that, Zuppke responded, "And all Galli-Curci can do is sing."

His was perhaps the first number immortalized in sports lore—Number 77.

"Zuppke always said the reason I got 77 was because the day they handed out the numbers I was standing between 76 and 78.

"I was an iceman back home in Wheaton, Illinois, all through high school, college, and even for a few years when I was with the Bears. Carrying those blocks of ice upstairs was great for the legs. Towards the end of my career I drove to the ice house in a $6,000 Lincoln and the fellow who owned the business said, 'Who's working for whom around here?'"

Grange was working for Halas. Together they made the Chicago Bears into the greatest team of pro football's early years.

"I played in the first three pro championship games," he said. "The first was 1932. We played the Portsmouth, Ohio, team, which later became the Detroit Lions. A big snowstorm came up and we had to move indoors into the Chicago Stadium. The only trouble was the stadium was only 80 yards long. So when a team reached the 50-yard line, it was automatically penalized 20 yards to make up for the missing 20. The sidelines were five feet of solid cement. The floor was concrete with six inches of dirt

and other fragrant material. You see a circus had been there the day before."

For winning, the Bears received $250. "The money has changed considerably over the years," he said.

"The players today are good, but I don't think they're any better than in my day. They're bigger, that's all. When I joined the Bears in 1925, the linemen averaged 235 pounds. Now, they go at least 260 or 270.

"People seem to try to make the game more complicated than it is. The team that blocks better and tackles better still wins. I haven't seen a new play since high school."

Red Grange retired in 1935 at the age of 32. He had broken into the clear for what seemed to be a touchdown but he was caught from behind by a lineman. "I knew then that it was time to say goodbye."

"He is three or four men rolled into one," Damon Runyon once wrote. "He is Jack Dempsey, Babe Ruth, Al Jolson, Paavo Nurmi, and Man o'-War."

If he wasn't all of those, he was a very big part of their era—the Roaring 20s, a time when America was carefree and spent a lot of its time heaping adulation on its sports heroes. None was bigger than the Galloping Ghost, Red Grange.

"Those were great years," he said. "Some of the finest writers and editors were building up sports right after World War I when people wanted to relax a little bit, when the country was ready to expand. Maybe it was all built out of proportion but I'm glad to have been a part of it."

VINCE LOMBARDI

No, Vince Lombardi never said, "Winning isn't everything, it's the only thing." But in talking about his life as a football coach in Green Bay, Wisconsin, he did say, "Winning is not a sometime thing here. It is an all-the-time thing. You don't win once in a while, you don't do things right once in a while, you do them right all the time."

Vincent Thomas Lombardi did things right all the time. In nine seasons as the head coach of the Green Bay Packers, his teams won 106 games and lost only 37; they won five National Football League championships; they won the first two Super Bowls and they gave the nickname Titletown, U.S.A. to their smallish hometown in northern Wisconsin. He took over a team that had won one game in 1958 and made them respectable with a 7-5 record in 1959. In 1960 they won the conference championship and in 1961, they won the league title. It took Vince Lombardi 20 years of coaching to get the job of running a pro team and when he got it, there was no stopping him.

"I'm no miracle man," he told Packer executives when he took over the team. But he did perform miracles for he did not make major changes in the team. Many of the players remained. What he did was change their attitude. And he changed the attitudes of so many coaches who followed him.

"I have never been connected with a losing team," he said on being hired. "And this shall not be the first. I hope to instill a winning spirit on the Packers in a lot less than five years. I am tremendously impatient."

He made some changes, cut a few players but found that his players could perform quite well. All they had to be taught was to work.

"We had to instill a desire to win. The holdovers had to be taught that victory was probable, not impossible. We got rid of those players who clung to the team's defeatist attitude."

Billy Howton, one of the Packers mainstays felt the first blow. "Billy was a fine end," Lombardi said, "but we felt he had the wrong attitude, so we made an example of him."

With a quarterback named Bart Starr, whom most others had given up on, a running back named Paul Hornung, whose Golden Boy image never meshed with Lombardi's but who always pleased the coach on the field, and a ferocious defense led by Ray Nitschke, the Packers quickly became the best.

And his players loved him. "He's fair," said Henry Jordan, a tackle. "He treats us all the same—like dogs."

Throughout his career, Lombardi never stopped talking about football, winning football, and life:

"Football is a symbol of what's best in American life, a symbol of courage, stamina, co-ordinated efficiency or team work. It's a Spartan game, a game of sacrifice and self-denial, a violent game that demands a discipline seldom found.

"Football is a game for madmen. In football we're all mad. I have been called a tyrant, but I have also been called the coach of the simplest system in football, and I suppose there is some truth in both of these.

"The perfect name for the perfect coach would be Simple Simon Legree.

"Only three things should matter to you—your religion, your family, and the Green Bay Packers, in that order.

"There's nothing you can do about fumbles except scream.

"Football is a game of cliches and I believe in every one of them.

"I don't care what everybody else says."

He was born in Brooklyn and had been a star player at Fordham in the mid-1930s, one of Fordham's famed "Seven Blocks of Granite." He went to law school but there was really only one profession for him so he became a football coach, beginning as a $2,000 a year assistant in 1939 at a high school in Englewood, New Jersey. He went to Fordham as an asistant coach in 1947 and then to Army, where he was an assistant to the legendary Earl (Red) Blaik.

"Whatever success I have had must be attributed to the 'old man'," Lombardi once said. "He molded my methods and my whole approach to the game. The unqualified superlative is precarious, but if there is a Number One coach of all time, it is Red Blaik."

After five years at Army he joined the staff of Jim Lee Howell with the New York Giants.

"Vince didn't completely understand pro football when he came here," said Frank Gifford, then a star halfback for the Giants. "We were showing him things in the beginning. But that changed very, very quickly."

After five years, the Packers came a-callin'. "I knew it was time to make a move, if I ever was going to make one."

He stayed nine seasons and after winning the second Super Bowl, he gave up coaching. "What I have to say is not without emotion," he said that day. "'I am in excellent health, but the corporate structure of the Packers places a big strain on a general manager-coach. It is impossible for me to do both jobs anymore." And so he quit ready to move into the executive's chair exclusively.

But the challenge wasn't the same and while he watched from above, Phil Bengtson led the team to a losing season, something Lombardi had never faced. But his replacement could never be comfortable with a boss who had been so successful at the job. When the opportunity came to remake the Washington Redskins in 1969 as he had the Packers a decade earlier, he took it. And what he said when he got to the Capital sounded remarkably familiar.

"I have no preconceived notions about the Washington players. Whatever happened in the past is in the past." The Redskins won seven and lost five. They had not had a winning record in 13 seasons. But Vince Lombardi didn't have the chance to perform his Green Bay magic in Washington. Before training camp the following summer he was taken ill with cancer and he died Sept. 3, 1970. At Lombardi's funeral, NFL Commissioner Pete Roselle eulogized the coach with these words:

"Those who will miss him the most are those who still had yet to play for him, who might have been taught by him, led by him and counseled by him."

JIM BROWN

Who is the greatest football player ever? If you stop and think about it, the answer is easy: Jim Brown.

In nine seasons in the National Football League, Brown set records for rushing and touchdowns. He retired at the age of 29 in 1965 to pursue an acting career, never having been truly "stopped" by anyone. He rushed for 12,312 yards and 126 touchdowns in 118 regular season games and he never missed a game because of injury. In the 1983 season, Franco Harris of the Pittsburgh Steelers and Walter Payton of the Chicago Bears got closer to Brown's career rushing records. But if either should break the mark, he will have taken many more games to do it. Brown truly stands alone.

"If you analyze things intelligently," he said, "my record speaks for itself.

"When I played, gaining 1,000 yards in one season was a great accomplishment." Indeed, for Brown's first four years as a pro, the NFL played a 12-game season. "Once they went to 14 games, gaining 1,000 yards didn't mean anything to me. Then when they went to the 16-game season in 1978 and still considered 1,000 yards the measure of a good season, I couldn't understand it.

"Football when I played, was at one stage. Now it's just at another."

And when Harris got closer to the record it became apparent that one major part of Brown's makeup had not changed: he still had the sports world's biggest ego and he talked of making a comeback.

"I have the greatest respect for Franco Harris, but he is just hanging around to try to break my record. Even if Franco breaks my record by 500 yards, I will come back."

Would any club be willing to take a chance on a 47-year-old runner who had not played football in more than 18 years? You never know. After all, Jim Brown was once the best.

He played football, basketball, baseball, lacrosse, and ran track in high school in Manhasset, Long Island, New York. At Syracuse University, he starred in football (he once scored 43 points by kicking and running in a game) and lacrosse, which he always considered his best sport. "Name the game and he'll play it like a pro in 48 hours," said his college lacrosse coach, Roy Simmons. "He could be all-America in anything from tiddly winks to football."

When Brown was graduated from Syracuse, he was drafted in the first round by the Cleveland Browns. He immediately became a star.

"We just put him in there and he played," said Paul Brown, coach of the Cleveland team. "From beginning to end he knew precisely what to do and did it. He belonged. It was as simple as that."

For Jim Brown, it was not quite that easy. "When I was a kid I used to have daydreams and say to myself, 'Jimmy Brown, all-America.' I finally made that, but this was even more. Here I was with fellows I'd been reading about all my life and idolizing. I couldn't quite picture myself playing with them."

Oh, how he played! As a rookie he rushed for 942 yards, including 237 in one game. He got better and better. In his second season, 1958, he set a league season record of 1527 yards.

And he liked to say he was successful as much for his mental abilities as his physical attributes.

"I always made it a practice to use my head before I used my body. I looked upon playing football as a businessman might: The game was my business; my body and mind were assets and injuries were liabilities."

He broke his running style down to three different forms:

"The Cut, Change Pace, and Run By"—A self-explanatory method of avoiding potential tacklers.

"The Limber Leg"—In which Brown offered a tackler his leg, then when man grabbed for it, he pulled it back and ran away.

"The High Step"—A lengthened, knee-lifted stride designed to prevent converging tacklers from grabbing both legs at once.

"In one-on-one situations," Brown said, "you break guys into categories. If he's a lineman and he's four yards away, you figure to put a good move on him and go around. A linebacker is quicker and therefore harder to fake. If he is three yards or less away, you drop your shoulder and struggle. If he's a small defensive back, you just run right over him."

Ouch. Jim Brown was 6-feet-2-inches and a rock-solid 230 pounds.

How did you stop Jim Brown? "Give each guy on the line an ax," said Detroit's Alex Karras. "Hang on and wait for help," said Giants' Sam Huff.

But while Brown was racking up yardage, he began to enjoy the game less and less. The Browns won the league championship in his rookie season but failed to equal that accomplishment for the next several seasons as their arch-rivals, the New York Giants, dominated the league. By 1962 he had had enough of the Browns' unimaginative style of play and threatened to quit unless Paul Brown was let go.

"We were just a mechanical club," he said. "We'd run a play and just stand there and wait for the guard to come in with another." The team's owner, Art Modell, got the message and fired Paul Brown, the only coach the team had ever had.

The next season, under Blanton Collier, Jim Brown had one of the most remarkable seasons a professional football player ever had—he set a season record with 1863 yards rushing and he scored 15 touchdowns. He was happy again. The Browns won the NFL title in 1964 and the conference championship in 1965.

"Any play that gained yardage was a good play as far as I was concerned," he said, "Most plays aren't designed for long runs; they're just after a crucial few yards, maybe even inches, for a first down.

"The best part of playing football is when you're on the field and your team is moving. And every player on the field knows that you're going to move the ball, and you're really hitting and you're not thinking about anything else except playing the game. You're playing well and you have eleven men who are acting as one. No jealousies, no complaints. Just the idea of the ultimate goal of scoring a touchdown. It's just a feeling that is quite great to have."

Following the 1965 season, Brown had a role in the movie, "The Dirty Dozen." When filming in England was delayed by the weather in that summer of 1966, Brown called a news conference on the movie set in England and announced that he was finishing the movie and would have to retire from football. The English weather did in a few weeks what no NFL defender had ever done—knocked Jim Brown out of the league.

"It was the right time to retire. You should get out on top. In the three years with Blanton Collier and Art Modell, I have been able to do all the things I wanted to do. Now I want to devote my time to other things."

TOM LANDRY

The Dallas Cowboys filed into a meeting room one night in the summer of 1972. Coach Tom Landry strode to the front of the room and said, "These are the 48 men I am taking back to the Super Bowl." Jean Fugett, a rookie, looked around the room and quickly counted players. There were 48. That was how he realized he had made the team.

That's the way Landry works—businesslike, understated but always with an eye on the future. Twenty five years after he took the post, he is the only coach the Cowboys ever had. He has been hailed as the most innovative mind in pro football.

But for all his success—including two Super Bowl championships—there are many who feel Landry has been too stoic, unemotional as he has guided and instructed the Cowboys. Landry feels his methods are vital to success.

"I learned early in sports," he said, "that to be effective, for a player to play the best he can play, is a matter of concentration and being unaware of distractions, positive or negative. I try to block out everything that distracts me. Even a big play, I blank it out. If you show emotion in competition, temporarily, you'll be ineffective. If you're disciplined enough, you don't get down when you're behind and you have a chance to create something positive."

Landry sees these qualities in two of his favorite athletes, neither of them football players.

"Look at Bjorn Borg or Jack Nicklaus. Those guys really concentrate. With the world on their shoulders, they're so absorbed with what they're doing."

The very quality that Landry sees as his strength has caused problems with such former players as Pete Gent, Duane Thomas, and Thomas (Hollywood) Henderson. But the coach has survived and thrived and made most of his players Tom Landry fans. He has even allowed some to see another side of the stoic stone face under the snap-brim hat.

Charlie Waters, an outstanding Cowboy defensive back, has recalled a Cowboy team meeting when he was still active. The Cowboys had played poorly in three straight games and Landry addressed his players. "Trying to express where we had gone wrong, he choked up, and I saw tears in his eyes," Waters said. "We weren't delivering and he felt like he couldn't reach us. You could see the frustration. He just left the room."

So which is the real Tom Landry: The "plastic man" Duane Thomas once characterized him as; the coach who is moved to tears by his inability to communicate; or the actor in TV commercials who is able to poke fun at himself?

Though many have analyzed, few have understood the personality of this man.

What is easily understood is his genius at the game. He invented the umbrella defense while still an active player with the New York Giants. The defense was the first formation designed to counteract sophisticated passing offenses. He taught his players how to read a key.

"Look at that linebacker," he said during a Cowboy film session. "When his right foot is back, he's blitzing; when his legs are parallel he is not." The Cowboys didn't miss a blitz that whole game.

Landry came to the Giants as a player after having graduated from the University of Texas. He quickly was given additional responsibilities by the Giants' coach, Jim Lee Howell. He became the team's defensive co-ordinator and coached the defensive unit after retiring as a player. Those Giants were one of the first NFL teams to glorify the defense and the defensive players. When Landry talked he always talked positively—be prepared and nothing will surprise you.

"Defensive football has become a highly developed science," Howell said, "and the Giants have the world's leading scientist in Tom Landry. He's the best defensive coach in the business."

Once he was questioned on one of his defensive maneuvers by a Giant. "What if," the player said, "the runner isn't there?"

"Don't worry," Landry replied. "He'll be there."

When the Cowboys came into the NFL in the expansion of 1960, they chose Howell's scientist. His first Cowboy team won no games. In 1966, the Cowboys won 10 games, lost three, and tied one. Since then they have not lost more than they have won in any season.

To keep the Cowboys on top has required some tough decisions. When Henderson became, well, too Hollywood for Landry, he was fired despite his all-pro stature at linebacker.

"This is it," said Landry. "It would not be to his best interest to try to come back here." Henderson never did.

When Tony Dorsett joined the Cowboys as the Heisman Trophy winner and the top pick in the NFL draft, Landry made him wait for his starting spot.

"You're dropping too many passes in practice," the coach explained to his star runner.

"I know," Dorsett said, "but I'll catch those passes in the games."

"You've got to learn to catch them in practice first," said Landry. Dorsett did and has been one of the league's most productive players ever since.

In 1978, Dave Anderson of The New York Times conducted an informal survey of all 28 NFL coaches on whom they thought was the best in their fraternity. Landry won.

"Landry is a great organizer," said Chuck Knox, then with Buffalo. "He is innovative with all his multiple formations. It takes guts to be innovative. And he's also had the longest tenure."

"Landry wins," said Red Miller, then with Denver.

For his part, Landry picked Don Shula of the Miami Dolphins.

But modesty is not always part of Tom Landry's makeup. There was the time the Cowboys suffered a disappointing and surprising defeat. In the team meeting following the game Landry began by saying, "I gave you a perfect game plan and you blew it."

JOE NAMATH

When Steve Young signed to play quarterback for the Los Angeles Express of the United States Football League in March 1984 the total value of his contract was reported to be around $40 million for 40 years. The numbers are staggering. However, that inflated price tag did not cause the same kind of stir as the $427,000, three-year contract Joseph William Namath signed with the New York Jets in January 1965. Similarly it is unlikely that Steve Young will startle the pro football world on the field or off it as Namath did.

Joe Willie. Joe Willie White Shoes. Broadway Joe. His nicknames had the style of a man completely at ease in his surroundings. No event was too big. No situation unmanageable. He went from Beaver Falls, Pennsylvania to the University of Alabama and when he was signed by Sonny Werblin, the impresario who owned the Jets, Joe Namath became a star. His contract was worth more than any previous player's contract.

"I believe in the star system," said Werblin. "It's the only thing that sells tickets. It's what you put on the stage or the playing field that draws people. When Joe Namath walks into a room, you know he's there. When any other high-priced rookie walks in, he's just a nice-looking young man."

Namath walked into the room at the height of a pro football war between the upstart American Football League and the well-established National Football League. His contract signaled the end of a polite war with a few border skirmishes. This was combat. When Namath signed, the sports world (and a good deal of the rest of the world, too) took notice. The contract drove up salaries; it gave the AFL a credible presence in its most important market and it created a star with the talent and charisma to make the league a success. Namath made his professional debut in an exhibition game in Lowell, Massachusetts in July 1965 and more reporters covered the event than had covered the AFL championship game the previous December. By June of 1966, the football war was over and the leagues prepared to merge. By January 1969, Namath had led the Jets to the championship of pro football in Super Bowl III.

"We're a better team than Baltimore," he said in interviews before that game in Miami against the Colts. He also had little regard for the Colt quarterback. "Earl Morrall would be third-string quarterback on the Jets. There are maybe five or six better quarterbacks than Morrall in the AFL."

Then, speaking before a Touchdown Club in Miami he spoke volumes about his confidence. "We're going to win Sunday. I guarantee it."

Final score: New York Jets 16, Baltimore Colts 7.

The AFL had achieved parity with its older brother. And in one game Joe Namath showed that when you put up, you don't have to shut up.

From the beginning of his pro football career, Namath always had to put up. Shortly after he signed, a man came up to him at a cocktail party and said, "Joe Namath, you got it made."

"No sir, I don't have anything made."

But he knew he could make it and he knew he would.

His coach at Alabama, the great Bear Bryant called him "the greatest athlete I've ever coached." That's quite a confidence-builder.

But there is always a sense of what-might-have-been with Namath. When he signed with the Jets he already had suffered his first knee injury and had surgery shortly afterwards. He had three more knee operations, a broken wrist, a separated shoulder, and numerous rib injuries, the result of not being mobile enough to get out of the way. His sense of humor was never damaged, however. He was once asked if the NFL should create rules to protect the quarterback.

"Nothing should be done to detract from the essence of the game—the fight to get at the quarterback, the fight between the offensive line and the defensive line. If the defense wins, you've got to give them their trophy.

"Their trophy is me."

And he knew that eventually his injuries would stop him from playing altogether. He once watched an elderly man being helped from a car on a crowded Manhattan street. After steadying himself on a fender the old man hobbled to the sidewalk.

"Must be an old quarterback," Joe Namath said.

Before Namath got to be an old quarterback, he spent a lot of time enjoying his life in the spotlight. He was America's most eligible bachelor

("I'd rather go to Vietnam than get married," he told his draft board). He had an East Side apartment with a white llama rug on the floor and mirrors on the ceiling. And he loved the nightlife of New York and he loved to be with beautiful women. He wanted what New York had to offer while he was still an undergraduate at Alabama. He wanted to "get to this town." When the Jets made their offer he took it although the St. Louis Cardinals of the NFL had offered almost as much.

But there was more to Joe Namath than a quick wit and a sense of bravado. He could play. He had a strong arm, a quick release on his passes, and an understanding of the way things worked. You didn't always have to look great. Results counted.

"I don't know how I throw the ball, and I don't remember anybody ever teaching me to throw it. But there's a lot I have found out."

Here's what he found out about his passing style:

"The quicker you get rid of the ball, the fewer times you're going to get caught with it—and the faster the ball gets to the receiver. I'd say I save at least two tenths of a second and probably even more than that on a pass play. That's worth a lot when you consider that on a pass play the quarterback would like to have four seconds from the time the ball is snapped until he throws it. You'd like to have four seconds but you don't always get it."

In 13 seasons, Joe Namath passed for 27,663 yards and 173 touchdowns. In 1967 he became the first quarterback to total more that 4,000 yards passing in a season. He played 12 seasons with the Jets and finished up with the Los Angeles Rams. He went to the Rams when his Jets' contract (by now worth $450,000 a season) ran out and he saw little future with the team and it saw little future with him. He switched coasts hoping for one more shot at the Super Bowl but he wound up second string and left the game for a career as an actor following the 1977 season.

He told the writers who doubted his prediction before Super Bowl III, "I hope all you guys eat your pencils and pads. We won."

And he told the world exactly how life according to Broadway Joe worked: "I wish I was born rich. I'd know how to spend money. Boats, planes, cars, clothes, blondes, brunettes, redheads, brownheads, just so they're pretty. I love them all. What's there in life but to relax and have some fun. Man, if you don't have it, you're not living and I like to live."

JOHN RIGGINS

"There are hundreds and hundreds of football players. A few stand out, even when they're doing almost nothing. John Riggins is one of those."

The speaker was Bobby Beathard and he should qualify as an expert on John Riggins for he is the general manager of the Washington Redskins, who Riggins plays for and led to the Super Bowl in 1983 and 1984. And there are several reasons John Riggins stands out: he is a running back with few peers and has been since 1971; he has sat out a full season in a dispute over his salary; he sued that team saying that he was owed a year's pay even though he didn't play; he showed up at training camps with the New York Jets sporting first a huge Afro and then a Mohawk haircut; and he appeared at a pre-Super Bowl party in white tie and tails.

There's more, but first listen to John Riggins talk about being an unorthodox athlete in the orthodox world of professional football.

"I'm just expressing myself," he says. "I like to do what I like to do at the moment. I'm spontaneous, but I like to think I'm always in control of the situation. I grew my Mohawk for the fun of it. I wanted to show everybody I was my own boss."

Everybody knows. But, of course, being his own boss hasn't kept Riggins from being one of the outstanding running backs in the history of professional football and one of the most durable.

He has been a pro running back for 13 seasons, including the one he missed with the Redskins in the salary dispute. Going into the 1984 season he had rushed for 9,436 yards in the regular season and an additional 916 yards in the playoffs. He had six straight playoff games with more than 100 yards rushing. But he takes all of that with a grain of salt and a smile.

"There are probably a few running backs who have been around for 12 years, but most of them are coaches."

But he understands what has made him a success. "When you run, you can't always get out of the line of force. But most of the time, I'm slipping punches. My running style is nothing special. It has been described as boring, which is probably true."

If his running style is boring, John Riggins never is. He is a product of the midwest—Centralia, Kansas, where he was one of three football-playing brothers, all of whom played at the University of Kansas. John was the biggest, the fastest, the best. He always did things a little differently.

"He's unique," his older brother Frank said. "What he does is what he is."

"He was that way in grade school, high school, everything." said his younger brother Billy. "He just did what he wanted to do. He's still unpredictable. I don't know what he totally thinks."

At the University of Kansas, he broke Gale Sayers's rushing records. He was a first-round draft choice of the New York Jets. Though he starred for the Jets and took a liking to living in Greenwich Village, he was never happy in New York and New York (the Jets at least) was never too happy with him. When he had the opportunity to leave the team as a free agent following the 1975 season he took it.

"The demand I put on the Jets," he said after signing with the Redskins, "was my way of saying, it's been nice."

But it wasn't always nice. While he was a Jet, Joe Namath, a fading Joe Namath, was a Jet. Though Riggins was the most important part of the Jet offense, Namath got the most money. Riggins had been a workhorse runner then, too, and he wanted to be paid for it. Perhaps not as much as Namath was getting but enough to signal the team's appreciation of his value.

"All the years I played football I've played scared," he said in 1973. "I always try to run around people although you have to run over people sometimes. You might say I've got a yellow streak, and I hope the Jets can paint it up with a little green."

They painted it a little, but not enough, and in 1976 John Riggins was a Redskin, made happy by the free-spending George Allen.

He moved on and found green pastures to go with the green stripe but he wasn't always happy with the way things worked in Washington, either. He signed a five-year contract with the Redskins but by the fifth season, he decided the Redskins should pay him more. The Redskins demurred. Riggins sat out the season back home in Kansas.

He returned before the following season announcing: "I'm bored, I'm broke, and I'm back." Then he stopped talking for most of that season. But what he found back with the Redskins was a new coach, Joe Gibbs, who had a new offensive formation—the one-back offense or the Ace. John Riggins was the Ace.

It took some time for Gibbs and his strategies to click and the Redskins lost their first five games in the 1981 season, but they won eight of the next eleven and the future looked bright. Even the fans had grown to love Riggins. When he returned, he said, "I expected to be treated like Public Enemy Number One." But that wasn't the case. The Redskins were getting good and Riggins was getting better.

The Redskins also had a group of young offensive linemen who named themselves the Hogs, a group of big young men who do their best work rooting around in the mud of pro football's trenches. Riggins became one of them, an honor he cherishes.

"We're blue-collar guys all the way," said Russ Grimm, an important Redskin lineman. "If we don't play football, we don't have any other job. Sure John's the highest paid guy on the team. But look at him—army boots and camouflage jacket, a typical blue-collar guy like us. He's no speedster, he's not one of those nifty runners. He's from the old school. John says, 'you block for me, I'll get some yards for you.'"

The Redskins went to the Super Bowl following the strike-torn 1982 season. And Riggins led the way. In Super Bowl XVII he set records for total yardage (166) and longest touchdown run (43 yards). Although Marcus Allen was to break those records the following year when the Raiders romped over the Redskins in Super Bowl XVIII, the memory lingers of what the big back from Kansas did that day in Pasadena.

He carried the ball 38 times. "That's on the verge of too many carries. I'm very happy but I'm very tired. I told Joe Gibbs that I wanted the ball before our playoff against Detroit. I think he got a little carried away."

With a runner like Riggins, why not get carried away? Even President Reagan did that day.

"I'm thinking of changing the spelling of my name to Reaggins," the President said in a telephone call to the winners' locker room.

Riggins, however, was his usual nonchalant self. "At least for tonight," he said, "Ron's the President, but I'm the king."

LAWRENCE TAYLOR

The quarterback was ready to take the snap from center. He leaned over and looked across at Lawrence Taylor, hoping to get a clue to what the defense might be doing. He looked again, thinking some movement by Taylor might tell if a blitz was coming. The quarterback's eyes met Taylor's.

Taylor smiled and winked.

"I know a lot of quarterbacks look over to see what I'm going to do," said Taylor. "There's a lot of eye contact. Sometimes I wink. The running backs smile when they see that. They know I'm coming on the play.

"They've still got to stop me. And maybe the quarterback will worry about me instead of what he's supposed to do. I try not to show when I'm rushing, but I guess I give it away. I get in a sprinter's stance. The coach says anybody can tell when I'm going to rush."

Well, the offense may know when Lawrence Taylor is going to rush, but after three seasons as a pro, no one has figured out how to stop him.

Taylor plays linebacker for the New York Giants. In his rookie season, he was named All-Pro, picked as the defensive player of the year, and the rookie of the year. The honors have not stopped coming. But he has not rested on his trophies. He doesn't even like to read about himself.

"If someone leaves a newspaper clipping about me, I kind of hide it because I don't like the other guys to see me caught up in that. After the season, a friend might bring out a scrapbook with a bunch of articles in it that I've never seen. I might read them, might not. I'm not interested in what people say about me now. I care what they will say when I leave the game."

When he leaves the game, everybody is sure to be talking with reverence. During Taylor's rookie season, the Giants asked their former center, Jim Clack, to come out of retirement. His number 56 had already been taken by Taylor.

"Jim Clack will have to wear another number," said George Young, the Giants general manager, "because Lawrence Taylor is going to take 56 to the Hall of Fame." For Taylor, it's no big deal. "All I'm doing is playing some ball and having some fun."

Some fun indeed. When Taylor was a rookie, the Giants made the playoffs for the first time in 18 seasons. Three victories were directly attributable to his play. In the final regular season game, he tackled Tony Dorsett, stripped him of the ball, and fell on the fumble. The Giants went on to make a game-tying field goal and then won in overtime.

But what manner of man is this 6-foot-2-inch, 242-pound paragon of ferociousness? Well, he relaxes by watching Three Stooges comedies and he is as amused by the reactions people have about him as by any of the antics of Moe, Larry, or Curly.

"In college at North Carolina, I was called Filthy McNasty, the Monster, Godzilla," he once said. "It didn't offend me. It didn't excite me either. You just chuckle at it and turn the page. My parents raised me to know myself. I'm like a big kid at heart. Someday, I'd like to own an amusement park with go-carts and all kinds of rides. I'd never get bored."

It didn't even take Taylor one quarter of a regular-season game to make his presence felt in the National Football League. While blitzing, Taylor ran into the Philadelphia Eagles quarterback Ron Jaworski just after he had released the ball. "Late hit," Jaworski shouted. "Where's the flag?"

"The flag's in the stands," the rookie shouted back.

Taylor has said that he had only one really good year and part of another as a college player. "Late in my junior year I began to get my act together. When people start noticing you some, that gives you something to live up to. I didn't want to let anyone down, especially myself."

He didn't. When George Young went to scout him during his senior year, Young was amazed. "With North Carolina's pale blue numbers, it's tough to pick out one guy from the other," he has recalled. "But I didn't need any numbers to locate Taylor. All you had to do was wait for a big defensive play to be made, and he'd be making it. It was hard for me to believe that a linebacker could so dominate a game."

The Giants had the second choice in the draft that spring. The New Orleans Saints had the first pick and chose George Rogers of South Car-

olina, the Heisman Trophy winner. The Giants were only too happy to take Taylor.

But for a while in January 1984, it looked as if the Giants might lose their star. He was wooed and won by Donald Trump, owner of the New Jersey Generals of the United States Football League. Taylor signed a huge contract with the Generals, then changed his mind and bought out his Generals' contract so that he could remain a Giant. Afterwards, Taylor talked football, 1984 style.

"I want to play for the Giants, but I also wanted to be treated fairly and now I'm being treated fairly. Hopefully, I'll take this Giants' number to the Hall of Fame."

JOHN MADDEN

No one has contributed more to the public's understanding of football than John Madden. First, as a coach with the Oakland Raiders and more recently, as a color commentator for CBS, Madden has talked football better than anyone.

When he started broadcasting, "The advice I used to get was to keep it simple. But I'd rather keep it understandable. The complexity of the game is what makes it so interesting."

Madden does a fine job at that. For instance: "Watch his left leg," he will tell viewers during a replay showing an offensive lineman missing a block. "That just opens the whole line."

Or an out-of-position defensive back: "This guy's taking a walk in the park. He's the one I'd be mad at."

Listening to Madden describe a football game on television is almost as much fun as it was watching him coach. You know he loves football and he'll do all he can to make you love it, too. "I've always been a teacher, even when I was coaching. I just take the information and present it in a way I hope people can understand."

Madden began coaching at the age of 23 when his football career was ended by a knee injury. He joined the staff of the Oakland Raiders in 1967 and became the team's head coach in 1969. At the age of 33 he was the youngest head coach in pro football.

He was one of the most successful coaches in pro football history. By the time he retired following the 1978 season, his teams had won 103 games, seven division championships, two conference championships and one Super Bowl. But for all that success, Madden always lived in the shadow of the Raiders' general-manager-genius, Al Davis. It was Davis who shaped the Raiders in the early days of the American Football League, made them a winner both as coach and later as the team's general partner.

But now in retirement from coaching, John Madden is one of the most recognizable faces in America. In addition to his duties as a broadcaster he has done a popular series of beer commericals. Using the same blustery style he favored while coaching, John Madden has become a star.

"They told me when I started doing the commercials that the exposure would be frightening. But I said, 'Me? I've been in the Super Bowl.' Well, they were right and I was wrong. I coached for 20 years, and then I break through one piece of paper for one 30-second commercial and everybody knows me as the guy who breaks through the paper."

He got into broadcasting (and advertising) when an ulcer and the pressures of coaching became too much. "The constant worrying made the seasons run together, and I just burned out."

George Blanda, who played pro football for 26 seasons, once said of Madden, "Of all the coaches I ever played for, John Madden was the kindest and most thoughtful." When Darryl Stingley, a receiver for the New England Patriots, suffered a paralyzing injury in an exhibition game against the Raiders, Madden spent part of the night at the hospital comforting the injured player.

"On the field we play hard," he said. "But when something like Darryl's injury happens, we're all in this game together."

Yet he also could feel for the man whose tackle injured Stingley, Jack Tatum. "In high school, they told him to hit hard, so he hit hard. At Ohio State, they praised him for hitting hard, so he hit hard. He became an All-Pro in the NFL for hitting hard. And then, after the accident, people changed the rules. Now he was evil for hitting hard.

"Football is a tough and violent game. When two big, strong, fast people collide, that's a violent act. People pay to see violence and then when someone gets hurt, they scream about it. That just doesn't make sense."

He loved the Oakland Raider crew of reprobates who sometimes did more training in a cocktail lounge than on the practice field. "Three things made Kenny Stabler great," Madden said. "He loved playing, he thought he was good, and he had no fear. I remember a playoff against Baltimore in 1977. It's overtime and we're on the sideline. I'm telling Kenny to throw Ghost to the Post (Dave Casper slanting over the middle) and he says, 'Know what coach?' I thought he was going to say something about how it wouldn't work. He cocked his helmet back, looked around the stands and said, 'These people sure are getting their money's worth.' "

The Raiders got their money's worth from Madden for two more seasons and then he said, "Enough."

Now all football fans are reaping the benefits of this love affair between Madden and the game. Between plays, he uses an electronic chalkboard to diagram what has just taken place, to help the viewer understand the reasons why things happen the way they do. He is critical when he thinks he has to be, and offers praise when it is due. He brings the flavor of the game from the field into the viewer's home.

A close-up of one player who has just done something good on the field shows him expectorating on the sidelines. Madden comments, "He even spits good."

A close-up of some tough offensive line play: "That was a good grunt contest. If we had a mike down there, we would have heard it."

He is always well-prepared.

"When I started in 1979, most people used to cruise in the night before a game and have cocktails with the teams' public relations guys. That was their idea of research." Now Madden and his broadacast partner, Pat Summerall, spend most of each week at the site of their game, talking to players and coaches, and watching films and practices.

"Football is like math," he says. "If you don't keep up, it runs away with you."

LESTER HAYES

It was January 1981 and the Oakland Raiders had just won Super Bowl XV. In the center of the Raider locker room, Bryant Gumbel of NBC was interviewing jubilant Raider players. Lester Hayes approached the microphone and stammered his way through what was probably the most painful interview in television history. Lester Hayes could not talk.

"I think I had cameraphobia," Hayes said. "If I got in front of the camera I just started talking faster and faster." The faster he talked the less intelligible it became. And people wanted to talk to Lester Hayes because he interecepted 18 passes in the regular season and the playoffs and established himself as one of the best cornerbacks in pro football. Hayes has continued to play just as well at cornerback but he has changed in other ways. Now he can talk.

It is January 1984 and Super Bowl XVIII Week is just beginning. There are interviews with the Los Angeles Raiders' players on the field at Tampa Stadium and Lester Hayes is one of the star attractions.

Someone says that the Seattle Seahawks' receivers looked scared when the Raiders beat the Seahawks in the American Conference championship game. Hayes looked up into the sun for a second as if he would find his answer in the sky and said:

"Looks are factual."

Now that's better than a simple "yes" isn't it?

But Lester Hayes didn't get to be the player you could always depend on for a quote without traveling a tough and painful road. After his excruciating experience after Super Bowl XV, Hayes decided to do something about his stammer.

"I had so many peaks and valleys," he said. "I could go for weeks at a time and be very fluent. But then there were the valleys and they were so baffling." After speaking normally for as many as six weeks at a time, Hayes would lapse into the horrific stutter. "I got fed up with the valleys.

I met a baseball player—a superstar—who told me about Hollins College, where he got rid of his stutter."

So he spent part of that offseason studying and training at Hollins in Roanoke, Virginia and by training camp the next summer he was much more fluent. And now, the things people hear!

On why he was taking his fishing pole with him to Super Bowl XVIII:

"I've studied the scientific schooling patterns of all South American fish. It's right now that the spotted sea trout and the spotted sea bass are spawning in Tampa. I know the psychology of fish spawning and fish thinking and the types of baits to use this time of year."

On why he watches so many hours of film of opposing players:

"The first axiom of war is know your enemy."

On why he has been so successful in the risky business of pro cornerbacking:

"I've tried to incorporate other cornerbacks' strong points into my style. Besides, I've got a receiver's mentality as far as pass patterns are concerned. That's my forte; recognition in flight."

Lester Hayes was born in Houston, Texas and always had pro football on his mind. He says he used to watch Tom Landry's television program and line up his toy soldiers in the pass patterns of the Dallas Cowboys. After playing as a receiver and a tackle in high school he went to Texas A & M, where he became a linebacker and then a safety. He was chosen by the Raiders in the fifth round of the 1977 NFL draft and was immediately switched to cornerback. He was not thrilled.

"I was really baffled at the logic behind the swich. I kept telling Al Davis I wanted to play safety. He kept saying 'You're going to be a good corner.'" Since Davis is the managing general partner of the Raiders and leaves his imprint on many of the football decisions, Hayes remained a cornerback. "I told myself in '79 there was no feasible way to play safety. So I just stopped asking. I wanted to be the best corner in the league. I told myself I wouldn't get beat."

He rarely gets beat. Even Lester Hayes listens to Lester Hayes.

He has been all-pro four straight years. In the first of those seasons, the year of the 18 interceptions, Hayes came into the spotlight for his use of a sticky substance called "Kwik Grip." He spread it all over his hands arms and uniform, hoping to get an extra edge in holding onto passes and pass receivers.

"If a pass comes to me," he said, "I won't drop it. You know you are what you think you are." Following that wonderful season, the use of sticky substances was banned by the league. Although his interception total has fallen off, that can be attributed as much to the quarterbacks not throwing his way as the banning of the goo.

He is now paired with Mike Haynes in a Raider defensive backfield many consider the toughest tandem in pro football history to throw against. Just ask Joe Theismann of the Redskins, who attempted it and failed as Washington lost to the Raiders, 38-9, in Super Bowl XVIII.

"Their cornerbacks played tough. They shut our wide passing game down. By them pressing our receivers so much, you had to be extremely accurate."

The Raiders acquired Haynes to go along with Hayes midway through the 1983 season. Hayes has spoken of his belief that he is a Jedi Knight, made popular in the "Star Wars" movie trilogy. When Haynes told Hayes at the 1983 Pro Bowl that he was about to become a free agent, Hayes "felt a tremor in the force." And sure enough when Haynes couldn't work out details of his contract with the New England Patriots, he was acquired by the Raiders. Said Hayes, "I think at times that I have soothsayer qualities. Fascinating."

Fascinating indeed. When asked why Mike Haynes would be so valuable in the Raiders scheme of things, Hayes said, "For seven years of his life, he has been frozen in carbonite. His legs are fresh now from playing all those zone coverages. Mike's 30 years old but Mike's body is that of a 24-year-old guy. There's not much wear and tear."

Before the Super Bowl with the Redskins Hayes gave his prediction on how the game would go.

"This game," he said, "is going to be a battle of two titans, two teams on the same mental par—pushing, shoving, biting, and scratching."

And when it was over and Hayes and Co. had done their damage to the highly technical Redskin offense, in particular the receivers known as the Smurfs, he said, "Going into the game, we planned to play about 45 percent man-to-man coverage. By the fourth quarter, that had changed to about 95 percent. Why? Because we knew that the Smurfs could not function properly with tight physical man-to-man coverage.

"We forestated the situation, and said we would score about 40 points. And we like to be accurate."

INDEX

Ace, 52, 126
Adderley, Herb, 62
AFL, 71, 83, 119, 131
Alabama, University of, 119, 120, 122
Albert, Frankie, 87
All-America, 7, 8, 112
Allen, George, 124
Allen, Marcus, 5, 6, 69, 126
Alley oop, 14
All the lights aren't on, 14
Alworth, Lance, 83
Ameche, Alan, 70
American Football Association, 10
American Football League, 71, 83, 119, 131
American Professional Football Association, 99
Anderson, Ken, 30
Anderson, Ottis, 72
Animal, 14
Army, 9, 95, 98, 108
Arnett, Jon, 17
At the door, 14
Audible, 15

Baab, Mike, 49
Babartsky, Al, 18
Baker, Gene, 91
Baltimore Colts, 41, 70, 77, 86, 120
Baugh, Sammy, 76, 83–84
Bears, Chicago, 30, 74, 87, 88, 99, 102, 103, 104, 111
Beathard, Bobby, 123
Bednarik, Chuck, 78
Bellard, Emory, 82
Bengtson, Phil, 110
Big Game, 11
Biletnikoff, Fred, 20
Bills, Buffalo, 65
Blaik, Earl, 108

Blanda, George, 132
Blistering, 15
Blitz, 16
Blue-chipper, 16
Bomb, 16
Bookend, 17
Bootleg, 17
Branch, Cliff, 80
Breakaway back, 17
Brick wall, 18
Bring in the chains, 18
Broken-field runner, 19
Broken play, 19
Brown, Jim, 11, 111–114
Brown, Paul, 48, 112, 114
Brown, Tom, 63
Browns, Cleveland, 48, 49, 73, 112
Bryant, Paul, 84, 120
Buffalo Bills, 65
Bull, 19
Bulldogs, Canton, 100
Bullet pass, 19
Bump and run, 19
Burner, 20
Butkis, Dick, 30
Buttonhook, 20

Cadence, 21
California, University of, 11, 88
Camp, Walter, 6, 8, 91–94
Campbell, Earl, 37
Canton (Ohio), 10, 99
Canton Bulldogs, 100
Cardinals, Chicago, 100
Cardinals, St. Louis, 78, 122
Carlisle Institute, 9, 10
Casper, Dave, 84, 132
Catlike, 21
CBS, 131
Center, 21
Chandler, Wes, 34

Chargers, San Diego, 52, 83, 86
Chicago Bears, 30, 74, 87, 88, 99, 102, 103, 104, 111
Chicago Cardinals, 100
Chip shot, 22
Chuck, 22
Circus catch, 22
Clack, Jim, 127, 128
Clark, Dwight, 33
Cleveland Browns, 48, 49, 73, 112
Clipping, 22
Clothesline tackle, 23
Coffin corner, 23
Collier, Blanton, 114
Colorado, University of, 89
Colts, Baltimore, 41, 70, 77, 86, 120
Columbia Broadcasting System, 131
Columbia University, 6
Containment, 24
Co-op blocking, 24
Cornell University, 65
Cornerback, 24
Counter play, 25
Cowboys, Dallas, 24, 37, 66, 86, 116, 117, 118, 136
Crackback block, 25
Crawling, 25
Cromwell, Nolan, 16
Crowley, Jim, 10, 96, 104
Curtis, Nathaniel, 91
Cut back, 26

Dallas Cowboys, 24, 37, 66, 86, 116, 117, 118, 136
Davis, Al, 131, 136
Decatur Staleys, 99
Delay, 26
Depth chart, 26
Detroit Lions, 49

Ditka, Mike, 74, 102
Dive play, 26
Dolphins, Miami, 118
Domination block, 27
Don't hit him, he's dead, 27
Doomsday Defense, 11
Dorais, Gus, 9, 95, 96
Dorsett, Tony, 43, 118, 128
Down, 27
Down and out, 28
Draft, 28
Draw play, 28
Drop back, 29
Drop kick, 29
Druze, Johnny, 18
Dump off, 29

Eagles, Philadelphia, 78, 128
Eat nails, 30
Eat the ball, 30
Encroachment, 30
End around, 31
End-over-end, 31
English, Doug, 49, 53
Express, Los Angeles, 77, 119

Face mask, 31
Fair catch, 31
Fears, Tom, 86
Fearsome Foursome, 37
Field goal, 32
Field position, 32
Fields, Greg, 77
Films, 32
Find the seam, 32
Fire out, 33
Fischer, Pat, 20
Flag, 33
Flag football, 33
Flanker, 33
Flare out, 33
Flat, 34
Flea flicker, 34
Flood the zone, 34
Flores, Tom, 5
Flowers, Charlie, 83
Fly pattern, 34
Flying wedge, 35
Fordham University, 18, 108
"40," 35
49ers, San Francisco, 14, 19, 87

Forward fumble, 35
Four Horseman, 10, 96, 104
Fouts, Dan, 57
Franco, Ed, 18
Free kick, 35
Free safety, 36
Freeze, 36
Front four, 36, 37
Fugett, Jean, 37
Fullback, 37
Fumble, 37
Fun Bunch, 11

Galloping Ghost (Red Grange), 100, 102, 103–106
Game, The, 11
Game plan, 37
Gamer, 37
Gang tackle, 38
Gap, 38
Gastineau, Mark, 37, 42, 61
Generals, New Jersey, 130
Gent, Pete, 115
Georgia Tech, 88
Get off the ball, 38
Giants, New York, 11, 28, 41, 70, 87, 103, 108, 114, 116, 127, 128
Gibbs, Joe, 52, 126
Gifford, Frank, 110
Gipp, George, 96–98
Go against the grain, 38
Goal-line defense, 38
Gogolak, Pete, 65
Go north and south, 39
Grange, Red, 100, 102, 103–106
Grant, Bud, 43
Green, Roy, 78
Green Bay Packers, 18, 62, 63, 71, 85, 107, 108, 110
Greene, Joe, 37, 84
Greenwood, L.C., 37
Grier, Roosevelt, 37
Grimm, Russ, 24, 126
Grind it out, 39
Guard, 39
Gumble, Bryant, 135
Guy, Ray, 23

Hadle, John, 77

Halas, George, 10, 87, 99–102, 103, 104
Halftime, 39
Hang time, 39
Hannah, John, 39
Harmon, Tom, 85
Harper, Jess, 96
Harris, Franco, 64, 111
Harvard University, 7, 91
Hash marks, 40
Hayes, Bob, 66
Hayes, Lester, 135–138
Haynes, Mike, 68, 138
Head hunter, 40
Hear footsteps, 40
Heffelfinger, Walter, 7, 9, 92, 94
Heisman, John W., 8
Heisman Trophy, 40, 69, 118, 130
Henderson, Thomas, 115
Hightops, 41
Hirsch, Elroy, 85
Hitch, 41
Hogs, 11
Hold and release, 41
Holding, 42
Hollins College, 136
Holmes, Ernie, 37
Hornung, Paul, 85, 108
Hot dog, 42
Houston Oilers, 14, 15
Howell, Jim Lee, 110, 116
Huddle, 42
Huff, Sam, 114

Iceman, 43
I formation, 43
Impact player, 43
Intentional grounding, 44
Interception, 44
Interference, 44
In the trenches, 43

Jacoby, Joe, 24
Jam, 45
Jaworski, Ron, 128
Jenkins, Alfred, 75
Jeter, Bob, 62
Jets, New York, 37, 42, 120, 122, 123, 124
Johnson, Billy, 42

Johnson, Pete, 26
Jones, Bert, 19
Jones, David, 37, 86
Jones, Ed, 86
Jordan, Henry, 108
Jump pass, 45

Kansas, University of, 124
Karris, Alex, 114
Keys, 45
Kivlan, James H., 94
Klecko, Joe, 37
Knee, 45
Knox, Chuck, 118
Kush, Frank, 77

Lamonica, Daryle, 80
Landry, Tom, 115–118, 136
Lane, Dick, 86
Lateral, 46
Layden, Elmer, 10, 96, 104
Limpoffs, 46
Linebackers, 46
Lions, Detroit, 49
Lipscomb, Gene, 86–87
Lockhart, Carl, 87
Lofton, James, 58
Lombardi, Vince, 18, 71, 107–110
Look in, 47
Looping, 47
Los Angeles Express, 77, 119
Los Angeles Raiders, 5, 28, 48, 80, 126
Los Angeles Rams, 17, 37, 86, 87, 122
Lundy, Lamar, 37
Lyons, Marty, 37

McBride, Mickey, 73
McElhenny, Hugh, 19, 87
Mack truck, 47
McNally, John, 87
Madden, John, 5, 131–134
Manster, 47
Man to man, 48
Marshall, George Preston, 102
Matson, Ollie, 17
Meat grinder, 48
Mehre, Harry, 7
Messenger, 48

Miami Dolphins, 118
Michigan, University of, 7, 8, 103
Miller, Don, 10, 96, 104
Miller, Red, 118
Minnesota Vikings, 62
Misdirection, 48
Mississippi, 88
Modell, Art, 114
Momentum, 49
Monday morning quarterback, 49
Monster back, 49
Monsters of the Midway, 11, 102
Montana, Joe, 33
Morrall, Earl, 120
Move the pile, 49
Muff, 50
Multiple set, 50
Munoz, Anthony, 27
Myra, Steve, 70

Namath, Joe, 11, 45, 71, 119–122
National Broadcasting Company, 135
National Football League, 10, 20, 42, 66, 70, 71, 79, 81, 86, 99, 100, 107, 110, 111, 116, 118, 119, 120, 122, 128, 132
NBC, 135
New England Patriots, 89, 132, 138
New Jersey Generals, 130
New Orleans Saints, 128
Newsome, Ozzie, 72
New York Giants, 11, 28, 41, 48, 70, 87, 103, 108, 114, 116, 127, 128
New York Jets, 37, 42, 120, 122, 123, 124
New York Sack Exchange, 11, 36, 37
NFL. *See* National Football League
Nickel defense, 50
Nitschke, Ray, 108
Nixon, Richard, 5
North Carolina, 128
North Texas State University, 84

Northwestern, 96
Nose tackle, 51
No shows, 50
Notre Dame, 7, 9, 10, 41, 85, 94, 95, 96, 104
Nutcracker, 51

Oakland Raiders, 81, 84, 89, 131, 132, 135, 138
Offsides, 52
Off-tackle, 52
Oilers, Houston, 14, 15
Olsen, Merlin, 37
One-back offense, 52
Onside kick, 52
Option, 53
Owens, R.C., 14

Packers, Green Bay, 18, 62, 63, 71, 85, 107, 108, 110
Paquin, Leo, 18
Patriots, New England, 89, 132, 138
Payton, Walter, 88, 100, 111
Penetration, 53
Philadelphia Eagles, 78, 128
Phillips, Bum, 14, 15
Pierce, Nat, 18
Piling on, 54
Pinching, 54
Pit, 54
Pitchout, 54
Pittsburgh Steelers, 84, 89, 111
Play action, 54
Playbook, 55
Play on a short field, 55
Plug a hole, 55
Plunkett, Jim, 41, 80
Pocket, 55
Polo Grounds, 103
Post pattern, 55
Powell, Marvin, 17
Power back, 56
Pressure, 56
Prevent defense, 56
Princeton University, 6, 7
Pro Football Hall of Fame, 76, 83
Pro Magazine, 25
Pulling guard, 57
Pull taffy, 56

Punt, 57
Purple People Eaters, 11
Put the hat on, 57
Pyle, C.C., 103

Quarterback, 57
Quarterback sneak, 58

Racehorse, 58
Raiders, Los Angeles, 5, 28, 48, 80, 126
Raiders, Oakland, 81, 84, 89, 131, 132, 135, 138
Rams, Los Angeles, 17, 37, 86, 87, 122
Read pattern, 58
Reagan, Ronald, 5, 126
Red-chipper, 58
Red dog, 58
Redskins, Washington, 5, 48, 52, 55, 76, 102, 110, 123, 124, 138
Release, 59
Reverse, 59
Reynolds, Jack, 88
Rice, Grantland, 10, 96
Riegels, Roy, 88
Riggins, John, 52, 123–126
Riley, Ken, 21
Ring the bell, 59
Rockne, Knute, 7, 9, 95–98
Rogers, George, 63, 128
Rollout, 60
Roosevelt, Theodore, 8, 35, 94
Rose Bowl, 7, 8, 88
Roselle, Pete, 110
Rouge, 60
Roughing, 60
Rover, 60
Royal, Darrell, 82
Running back, 61
Run to daylight, 60
Rutgers University, 6
Ruth, Babe, 100

Sack, 61
Sack Exchange, 11, 36, 37
Safety valve, 61
St. Louis Cardinals, 78, 122
Saints, New Orleans, 128

San Diego Chargers, 52, 83, 86
Sandwich, 61
San Francisco 49ers, 14, 19, 87
Salaam, Abdul, 37
Sayers, Gale, 88, 124
Scramble, 61
Screen pass, 62
Scrimmage, 62
Seahawks, Seattle, 135
Seam, 63
Secondary, 62
Selmon, Lee Roy, 56
Senior Bowl, 88
Seven Blocks of Granite, 10, 18, 108
Seven Mules, 10, 96
Shank, 63
Shaughnessy, Clark, 74
Shed a tackler, 63
Sheets, Ben, 86
Shotgun, 63
Shula, Don, 118
Single wing, 63
Situation substitution, 64
Skirt the end, 64
Slant, 64
Slot, 64
Smith, Holden, 77
Smurfs, 11, 138
Snap, 65
Soccer-style, 65
South Carolina State, 86
Southern California, University of, 69
Spear, 65
Special teams, 65
Speedo, 66
Spike, 66
Spiral, 66
Split, 67
Split the uprights, 67
Springs, Ron, 81
Squareout, 67
Squib kick, 67
Stabler, Ken, 80, 88, 132
Stagg, Amos Alonzo, 92, 94
Staley, A.E., 99
Staleys, Decatur, 99
Stanford University, 8, 11, 41
Starr, Bart, 29, 108
Staubach, Roger, 78
Steel Curtain, 37

Steelers, Pittsburgh, 84, 89, 111
Stenerud, Jan, 32
Stop and go, 67
Stingley, Darryl, 89, 132
Straightarm, 68
Strip the ball, 68
Strong safety, 68
Strong side, 68
Student-body right, 69
Stuhldreher, Harry, 10, 96, 104
Stutter step, 69
Submarine, 69
Sudden death, 70
Sugar Bowl, 88
Suicide squad, 70
Summerall, Pat, 5, 134
Super Bowl, 5, 6, 14, 63, 71, 81, 107, 110, 115, 120, 122, 123, 126, 131, 132, 135, 136, 138
Swann, Lynn, 22
Sweep, 72
Swim, 72
Swing pass, 72
Swivel hips, 72
Syracuse University, 112

Tackle, 72
Tailback, 73
Tank, 73
Tarkenton, Fran, 62
Tatum, Jack, 84, 89, 132
Taxi squad, 73
Taylor, Lawrence, 11, 46, 127–130
Tennessee, University of, 88
Tennessee State, 86
Texas, University of, 82, 116
Texas A&M, 82, 136
T formation, 73–74
Theismann, Joe, 40, 41, 138
Thomas, Duane, 115, 116
Thorpe, Jim, 9, 10, 100
Throw into a crowd, 74
Throw it away, 74
Tight end, 74
Tightrope, 75
Tingelhoff, Mick, 21
Tittle, Y.A., 14, 41
Touchback, 75
Touchdown, 75

Touchdown Twins, 10
Touch football, 75
Trap, 75
Triple-threat back, 76
Tunnell, Emlen, 87
Turk, 76
Turn in, 77
Turn it over, 77
Two-minute drill, 77
Two-minute warning, 78
Two-way player, 78

Underneath, 79
Unitas, John, 41
United States Football League, 10, 77, 119, 130
University of Alabama, 119
University of California, 11, 88
University of Colorado, 89
University of Illinois, 103
University of Kansas, 124
University of Michigan, 7, 8, 103
University of Southern California, 69
University of Tennessee, 88
University of Texas, 82, 116
University of Washington, 87
Upright, 79
USFL. *See* United States Football League

Veer, 79
Vermeil, Dick, 32
Vertical passing game, 80
Vikings, Minnesota, 62
Vow boys, 10

Walker, Herschel, 35
Walls, Everson, 24
Ward, Chris, 17
Washington, University of, 87
Washington Redskins, 5, 48, 52, 55, 76, 102, 110, 123, 124, 138
Waters, Charlie, 116
Weakside, 80
Wedge, 80
Wells, Warren, 80
Werblin, Sonny, 119
White, Byron, 89–90
White, Dwight, 37
White, Randy, 47
Widener College, 42
Wide receiver, 80
Wiggin, Paul, 11
Wild card, 81
Wingback, 81
Winslow, Kellen, 59
Wishbone, 82
Wojciechowicz, Alex, 18
Wood, Willie, 62

Yale University, 6, 7, 91, 92
Yeomans, Bill, 79
Yost, Fielding, 7, 8
Young, George, 128
Young, Steve, 10, 119
Younger, Tank, 73

Zone, 82
Zuppke, Bob, 100, 103, 104